I0760150

The People's Story of the Great Fire of London

To my old friend Bob Howells who, in the 1960s, wandered around London's East End with me, climbed the Pudding Lane monument and took in the massive chambers of St Paul's. Neither of us had any idea that the experience would ever take book form. It's taken time, old friend, but here it is.

As with everything I write, this is also for my darling Trudy. God bless you, sweetheart, wherever you might be.

The People's Story of the Great Fire of London

The Destruction of England's Capital City

Phil Carradice

First published in Great Britain in 2025 by
Pen & Sword History
An imprint of Pen & Sword Books Limited
Yorkshire – Philadelphia

ISBN 978 1 03611 697 2

A CIP catalogue record for this book is
available from the British Library.

Typeset by Mac Style
Printed in the UK by CPI Group (UK) Ltd, Croydon, CR0 4YY.

The Publisher's authorised representative in the EU for product safety is Authorised Rep Compliance Ltd., Ground Floor,
71 Lower Baggot Street, Dublin D02 P593, Ireland.
www.arccompliance.com

For a complete list of Pen & Sword titles please contact:

PEN & SWORD BOOKS LIMITED
47 Church Street, Barnsley, South Yorkshire, S70 2AS, England
E-mail: enquiries@pen-and-sword.co.uk
Website: www.pen-and-sword.co.uk
or
PEN AND SWORD BOOKS
1950 Lawrence Road, Havertown, PA 19083, USA
E-mail: uspen-and-sword@casematepublishers.com
Website: www.penandswordbooks.com

Wherever possible, I have retained the original spelling when quoting from primary source material of the later Stuart period. This is particularly the case with writers like John Evelyn and Thomas Vincent who appear to have their own distinctive idea of spelling and grammar.

Samuel Pepys has been published and re-published so many times that his words now have a distinctly twenty-first century appearance and feel to them – but even his diary entries are sometimes presented in their original form. Bear with me.

Contents

Introduction

Seminal moments in British history are many and varied. And yet, it is not those crucial moments themselves that tend to stay with you. Regardless of the events, do we really remember how the Gunpowder Plot was foiled or the Battle of Hastings won by the Normans? It is the lives and times of certain characters, the people involved, that stick most solidly in your mind. So, Guido Fawkes, King Harold, William the Conqueror and so on are the men who define the action and demand our attention.

The significance of any particular incident or its intricate details are important but they pale into insignificance when compared to characters who are a crucial element in whatever period of history that we are looking at. People, characters, call them what you will, are a crucial element in our study of our chosen subject.

They are an element that is that is often misinterpreted, often incorrectly described or simply men and women whose motives are questioned and misinterpreted. Think about it and consider just some of the great events in our history.

Start with the details and manoeuvring of ships during the Battle of Trafalgar. Do you know which ship moved which way and for what purpose? Probably not – and probably nobody does unless they are specialists in naval history.

But the death of Admiral Horatio Nelson and his famous final words? 'Kiss me, Hardy' or 'Kismet,' it hardly matters. Whether those last words are true or false, they stick in the memory and make the death of Nelson – his demise at the point of victory – all the more poignant and memorable.

Then you have the Battle of Hastings, the various charges by the Norman cavalry, the use of archers, the tactics of the English fyrd or infantry, the effect of the previous Battle of Stamford Bridge on battered limbs and so on. Only very rarely do most people get to know about them. What they do tend to remember, of course, is the totally inaccurate death of King Harold, courtesy of the Bayeux Tapestry and an imaginary arrow in the eye.

And how about Queen Elizabeth's stirring speech before the Defeat of the Spanish Armada in 1588? You might not know the words but you probably remember the sentiment – the body of a weak and feeble woman and so on. The speech was actually given after the Armada's defeat, when the Spaniards had been blown away to the north and victory assured for the English sailors.

Whoever and whatever you remember, it is the story of the people and the events they carry with them that drives our memories, makes them part of our understanding. The old writer's adage that all stories require the three p's – place, people, problem – remains true in factual accounts as well as in works of fiction.

Of course, people cannot stand alone. A sense of place will ground the story, particularly in events like the Great Fire of London. A powerful problem will hold the reader and the audience. But the real strength of any tale comes from the people, the characters, and the way they react to the place and the problem.

Stories make our history enjoyable and memorable. They are what we learn from. We gain very little from lists of dates or a relay of monarchs and their achievements. But that is exactly what most of us were given in our school history lessons: long lists and facts that really meant very little.

The Great Fire of London, a raging inferno that destroyed so much of the original and medieval city, is a classic case of the event being filled out, made more grounded and real, by the lives and actions of the people who were there. People make the story more impressive, more powerful, than the bare bones and facts of the event.

The names and characters of the main participants, men and women who were at the forefront in dealing with the fire, have been largely forgotten or deliberately ignored. Yet they remain an essential part of the story.

Diarists like Samuel Pepys and John Evelyn, ranting Puritan ministers like Thomas Vincent, even King Charles II and his brother James, Duke of York feature strongly in my understanding of the Great Fire of London. They were and still are central to the tale, dynamic and determined individuals, good and bad in their intentions, and essential elements in the story of one of the greatest dangers ever faced by the residents of London.

I ask, unapologetically, how many would-be readers of this book know the stories of those characters or can relate to their experiences? I would guess very few. How many readers know that both King Charles and his brother, the future King James II, were often up to their knees in water, helping to extinguish the fire? How many know what Pepys did with his valuable wheel of Parmesan cheese when fire threatened his house and his family?

Then there are Lord Mayor Thomas Bludworth and the deranged French martyr Robert Hubert, both of whom rose briefly to fame, not necessarily for the right reasons. There is the baker Thomas Farriner, owner of the property where the Great Fire began, the man who many believed was responsible for the disaster. Or the sailor and the soldier who beat out the flames on the roof of the Inner Temple and saved both lives and property?

How many have ever heard of preachers and prophets like Humphrey Smith and William Lilly? The list is virtually endless. Their involvement was immense but they have only rarely featured as significant figures, main characters in a drama of life, death and destruction.

I make no apologies for using these and other characters as the lynchpin from which the story of the Great Fire of London truly hangs. They were there, they experienced it, and they are the central focus of this book.

Pepys, King Charles and the rest, they walked the blazing streets, saw the burning houses, gave opinions at the time and, later, at leisure, opinions that could not be ignored. Through their words the sense of glory dying remains strong as the city they loved burned and perished before their eyes. Their affection is what gives the sense of place a deeper dimension.

Seminal moments need to be reinforced by, if there is such terminology, seminal people. That way lies interest and appeal. That way lies accurate history.

Chapter 1

Before the Blaze

Water was crucially important to the citizens of London in the autumn of 1666. Significant as it might have been for the ordinary members of the public, it was hardly a matter of importance to the national government or even members of the Corporation of London.

In 1666 the provision of reliable water supplies, like so many other essentials for living, rested in the hands of individual communities and parishes.

The late seventeenth century was an age when central authority was both limited and resented. That attitude was something of a hangover, the last remnants of ill feeling after the recent clash between Parliament and Crown in the Civil War.

The war had affected everyone, whichever side they supported. Anti-royalist emotion was still strong in cities like London, lingering in the breasts of the population following the recent internal conflict and the subsequent Commonwealth that shackled England in the grip of Puritan law and tradition. Events like a major fire or even an outbreak of a pandemic such as the plague were invariably dealt with on a local level, sometimes even on an individual basis, rather than through government intervention. It was an accepted process or reaction.

Water supply in 1666 was important for many reasons. It had been a long, hot summer, aggravating and annoying for anyone living in London, where the heat and stench of the city had become almost unbearable. There were no community bathing pools or baths just the muddy, silt-ridden Thames where dead animals, sewage and refuse competed against each other for sovereignty. There were not many citizens who would risk swimming or bathing in such a contaminated river. The Church was opposed to total immersion and, consequently, how to get and stay cool remained important issues.

And yet sweaty armpits and bad body odour were hardly the end of the world. That summer, the perceived low level of rain and river water in the city aqueducts and reservoirs was undoubtedly troubling. The non-appearance of rain clouds in the warm August and September skies offered potential problems. Rain clouds meant a break in the hot weather, something everyone in the city longed for on a daily basis. That was important to the populace but no more infuriating than the price of bread and corn going up.

The lack of an adequate water supply was something which was, initially at least, important but certainly not a major issue, either for the citizens or for the local authorities. There was enough to supply the people with drinking water – that was all that mattered.

Two huge wheels below London Bridge regularly pumped supplies to a water tower at Cornhill and then, by a system of elm pipes, to dozens of houses and shops in the north-eastern suburbs of the city. As well as ponds and streams, new reservoirs at Islington held fresh water from the rivers of Hertfordshire, nearly fifty miles away.

Regardless of the heat – and there was no denying the oppressive nature of it – to the casual observer the city was, it seemed, well supplied with water. All it needed was a little extra rain to fill the cisterns and reservoirs.

Dealing with community problems had always been a significant task for the aldermen and parish officials. Water shortages had been dealt with before and the parish councils had taken due note. For the moment at least, there was enough to supply people's basic household needs. The Thames would never run dry and so trade, the lifeblood of the city, would continue.

Potentially, as in any town or city where the buildings were made primarily of wood, there was always the danger of fire. The Corporation of London, like so many other town governing bodies, took a laid-back approach to the issue. Fire? Not a problem: deal with it when and if it happened.

It was a laissez-faire attitude, a self-indulgent belief that any country which had successfully passed through the rigours of a brutal civil war and killer epidemics like the Black Death, smallpox, and the sweating sickness would not be unduly bothered by a few sparks of fire.

The fact that wooden houses, lined with wattle and daub and crowned with straw roofs, made perfect fuel for fire somehow seemed to escape everyone. Previous fires in the city were a matter of history. Now the serried ranks of houses and churches dominated the skyline and all was well with the world. Fires might break out but that would happen somewhere else. Certainly not in London.

There was, of course, no such thing as a fire brigade in the city. Fighting fires was a clear case of action by the citizens for the safety of their fellow residents. The standard procedure in the event of a fire was simple. First, the alarm would be given, muffled church bells ringing backwards as the process was called.

The next stage was to block off the affected area or street and allow householders to form themselves into two separate lines. One line would pass empty buckets down to the Thames, while the other would pass full ones back up the street towards the fire. It was a sensible enough process but it did demand the co-operation of London's citizens.

Leather buckets and long ladders were available, usually stored in the parish churches. Also available for use were scoops and squirts, their names telling everything about their purpose, along with long fire hooks for pulling down burning buildings. The creation of such fire breaks was considered essential, in order to stop the flames spreading from one building to another.[1]

There were also an increasing number of new inventions in use in the city – in particular, new-fangled machines known as fire engines. Not all parishes possessed one as fire engines were fiendishly expensive to buy and difficult to use. They were usually mounted on sledges and pulled by gangs of twenty or so men or, occasionally, by horses through the city.

That process was fine on level streets but almost impossible on London's cobbled and pebbled walkways. The streets were so narrow that in many instances it was impossible to run a fire engine along them. It was another problem to be dealt with in the future. In 1666 local parishes invariably fell back on human involvement like the chain gang of bucket handlers. That was safe and familiar.

Until, that is, the coming of Armageddon changed everything. The outbreak of the Great Fire of London soon after midnight on 2 September 1666 halted the laid-back school of opinion, marking and securing it dead in its tracks.

The availability or scarcity of water was not the sole cause of the Great Fire, nor was it the main weapon in fighting it. But it played a part, a hugely important part, in what was to become the worst natural disaster ever to hit Britain's major community and commercial centre.

Personal loss or injury had always been accepted and then conveniently shelved and ignored. Damage and injury were inevitable in an outbreak of fire. The official line might be left unsaid but it was simple enough – you will lose property and possessions, accept that as a fact. Now let's get on with fighting the fire. You know the routine.

It was a concept and a practice that was all well and good for minor outbreaks but when an event like the Great Fire erupted the one thing that really mattered was the provision of decent leadership. Sadly, from the first flickering flames of the Great Fire, the almost total lack of leadership would become a serious issue.

If events got out of control, as they did on 2 September, the Lord Mayor, as the city's principal magistrate, was expected to take control but that demanded his presence on the scene. Just as there was no fire brigade, there was also no police force, only parish constables who were usually old men, well past their prime. Little better than watchmen, the safety and security of the city lay firmly in the hands of these men.

If the Lord Mayor was to handle the firefighting, he would first have to be informed and summoned. And for that to happen, the parish constables would have to have their own view of the seriousness of the situation. Once he had been informed, whatever action was required was down to the Lord Mayor. Arguably, it was a system that was designed to allow 'passing of the buck' at all levels of intervention.

That September, delay followed delay, and ineptitude wallowed in the footsteps of inadequacy. And it can be argued that right from the beginning, disaster was lurking in the shadows, waiting to strike out at an unsuspecting and self-satisfied populace. Mayhem and mischief were elements that were soon being played out.

The participation and leadership of Sir Thomas Bludworth, that year's Lord Mayor, is now remembered for his inadequacy rather than for any direct action he might, or might not have taken. It was a criticism that began on the first morning of the fire and grew to envelop the whole safety system of the city of London.

Add in a few totally inappropriate comments from the fumbling brain of Sir Thomas – who was, incidentally, London's 300th Mayor – and you find in the personality of the civic leader a weak man who laboured under severe pressure and stress.

It was hardly the way he would have wanted to be remembered, but Bludworth's ill-judged opinions and statements were to ensure immortality for the fire and for the man himself.

* * *

Despite their ineptitude, Bludworth and his cronies undoubtedly filled one element of the three essentials required in any effective story, factual or fictional – people or, as dramatists would have it, characters. The fire and how to extinguish the blaze were obviously the second requirement – problem. That leaves just one more essential factor – place.

Whatever its faults, by the 1650s and 1660s London was a thriving, rumbustious place, the largest community in England, the third largest in the western world. With a population of somewhere between 300,000 and 400,000 citizens, by the time of the restoration of the monarchy in 1660 the city boasted the largest market and the busiest port in Britain. Its wealth and success were based on trade, on commerce and on manufacturing.

The number of people living in London in the sixteenth and seventeenth centuries cannot be accurately calculated. The total was something of a changeable feast as migrants from Europe and from far distant parts of the British Isles were regularly moving into and out of London with little permanent record of their coming and going. Even now, in the view of many, there remains a belief that the upper estimate of 400,000 is too low.

What is clear, however, is that by the time of the Black Death in 1665 and of the Great Fire of London a year later, almost 80,000 people were living and working within the confines of the old city itself. The old city was just one part of London, comprising an area to the east of the seventeenth-century community, a well-established port and trading base. In 1666 it was bounded by the walls of the original Roman city. These still stood on the northern, eastern, and western sides of the enclave, the River Thames providing a barrier to the south.

This first settlement, predating the Roman occupation of Britain by many years, sat easily on the banks of the Thames. What the Romans created was Londinium, a relatively small community, covering a total area of just under 700 acres. Small it may have been, but the original city was ideally placed for trade and commerce and by the time the Romans left Britain in the fifth century it had become the most important economic centre in the country.

That position and status remained throughout the medieval period. Staying true to the Roman view of Londinium as a trading base, by the seventeenth century the old settlement, a city within a city behind its sturdy walls, had developed its position as the commercial heart of the metropolis. More importantly it had doubled, perhaps even trebled in size, both in land mass and in population.

However, its development had always been piecemeal, with the economic status and intent of the city being the one guiding factor. Buildings and living space had been totally unplanned, with the result that houses, shops and warehouses sat virtually one on top of the other. A perfect example of an anomie society gone drastically wrong, it was nothing short of a disaster waiting to happen.

Had they been blessed with the ability to travel through time, the Romans would not have recognised the city they had spawned. The greater community of London had expanded steadily since their days, sprawling out beyond the ancient walls, particularly to the west and north, where by 1666 badly built properties lined Fleet Street and what is now the Strand. Warehouses, shops, dwelling places, and businesses small and big stretched along the road and, significantly, crowded the riverbank towards the royal palace at Whitehall and Westminster Abbey.

The waterfront was the most dangerous and unplanned of all the newer London districts. In warehouses and in open courtyards, stacked in row after row along the wooden walls and fences, were barrels of highly flammable materials such as tar and pitch. Supplies of rope and canvas sails added to the risk of fire. Incredible as it might seem, in some of the warehouses there were even large supplies of gunpowder, left over from the recent civil war, along with fuses and matches. Ships, also carrying gunpowder and shot, called regularly at the quays and jetties of the district, their daily arrival and departure merely adding to the danger.

The city, old and new sections alike, comprised narrow streets and winding alleyways. The houses which lined the walkways were invariably built with straw roofs and constructed from a muddy and glutinous material called wattle and daub.

In itself, wattle and daub was a building material that was both resilient and relatively flame-resistant – until, that is, it became wet and damaged. If the outer coating of daub fell away, as often happened in the poorer parts of cities like London, it was nothing short of lethal. When nobody cared to repair or replace it, then the wattle was exposed, sometimes for months, even for years. And then it became a major fire risk.

Over the years there had been many edicts and proclamations prohibiting the building of wooden houses. Dwellings built of bricks and stone, the various parishes declared, were to be built instead. Unfortunately, brick and stone were hugely expensive and by the time of the Great Fire the only new buildings not made of wood and wattle and daub were the parish churches, public buildings, and the homes of a few rich merchants.

In the past, the old Roman walls may have withstood threats from native British tribes and other enemies, but that was a different age. Developments during the medieval period, along with modern post-Tudor and early Stuart economic structures, were a different matter altogether. Social changes were dramatic, the expectations of householders now being far more intense and demanding than they had been in Tudor times and before.

We might regard these expectations as normal or natural but little things like running water, cooking facilities within the house, and coal and wood fires in every room in order to give warmth had, by the time of Charles II, become almost commonplace. Luxury outweighed safety and the dangers inherent in such pleasures were not really recognised.

As London developed, small settlements sprang up around the new and original city. Shoreditch, Clerkenwell, Holborn and many other villages that are now regarded as an integral part of the city of London were originally totally separate communities.

Suburbs also developed to the south of the river, places like Southwark and Bermondsey, connected after 1209 to the rest of the city by the massive nineteen-arch London Bridge. The bridge was an impressive structure, regarded at the time as one of the wonders of English architecture and building expertise. Rows of wooden houses lined the bridge across the Thames and in all of them, as in the city itself, the danger of disaster was very real:

> The inherent difficulties for preventing accidental blazes were enormous, for all householders required fire for lighting, heating and cooking, and tradesmen such as bakers, brewers, tallow-chandlers, distillers, dyers, maltsters, soap-boilers, potters, and blacksmiths had to have ovens and furnaces on their premises.[2]

Open fires were the only way to heat buildings and most houses had at least two open hearths in each room. The fires in the grates were rarely extinguished, not even tamped down before the householders headed off for bed. Candles were often left burning all night and all day in the gloomy, darkened buildings. They were often left in the most inappropriate of locations, under stairs, on window sills and on crowded shelves of books, papers and other flammable materials.

Inns and taverns abounded in London, as might be expected in a city that survived by trade and manufacturing. These businesses offered warmth and comfort but they were also the providers of immense fire risks. Those risks were due largely to the supplies of hay and alcoholic spirits stored in their sheds and outbuildings.

The recent addiction to pipe smoking amongst male customers and travellers was another problem. This was particularly the case when the smokers paused to knock out the ash from the bowls of their pipes onto the wooden floor, rarely bothering to stamp out the embers.

Inevitably there were fires in the traffic-clogged, over-populated tenements of London. Most of them were relatively small, minor in nature and easily put out. Not all, however.

The earliest recorded instance of a significant fire was in 60 AD, when the forces of Queen Boudica burned the place to the ground. Two great medieval fires virtually destroyed the city in 1133 and 1212 but the most recent outbreak took place when what was then known as the Great Fire of 1653 erupted and burned down dozens of properties. Rebuilding was badly thought out and equally badly implemented.

In virtually every part of London, houses encroached onto the roads and alleyways, making transport and travel very difficult. Even walking was difficult on the crowded, dirty roadways. The practice of jettying, building or extending upper storeys out over the street, gave the city a claustrophobic feel and was also downright dangerous.

It is no exaggeration to say that men or women on one side of the street were able to lean out of their upstairs windows and shake hands with their neighbours on the other side of the road. The process of jettying also helped any conflagration jump from one side of the street to the other, spreading a blaze that could be fatal and seemingly unquenchable.

Disease, too, was seemingly unquenchable. London was an unhealthy place for residents and, for that matter, for visitors as well. With medical care still at a primitive level there was little effective treatment for serious disease and ailments.

Bubonic plague first appeared in Britain in 1348, a totally new pandemic that wiped out 3 million people, half of the population. This first epidemic raged across the country for just over two years before dying away early in 1350 but was guaranteed to return to crowded cities like London on an almost annual basis.

The regular annual arrival of the plague continued throughout the medieval period, reaching its climax with the outbreak which hit the city in May 1665. By that time what can be called herd protection or herd immunisation, in effect a familiarity with the disease, meant that the death total was not as severe as the original visitation.

Even so, by August that year a total of over 4,000 deaths a week was striking terror into the hearts of residents and virtually paralysing trade. In total, over 100,000 London residents, 15% of the city's population, died in that year alone. The disease spread easily from house to house, from person to person, and was inevitably soon carried to other parts of the country.

With the coming of winter in 1665, outbreaks of the plague finally began to die away and London residents heaved a combined sigh of relief. Their trials and tribulations were over, for a few months at least. They did not know what awaited them.

* * *

The days of excessive Puritan control had disappeared in the wake of the Restoration of the Monarchy. However, Puritanism was far from dead and Puritan preachers regularly regaled their congregations with tales of an angry and vengeful God who was preparing to take his revenge on the city and its residents. For most people specific examples of God's anger were difficult to identify but as far as the Puritans were concerned, he had a great deal to be angry about.

The Restoration of Charles II in 1660 was a moment of profound change. Almost overnight the style and management of government became very different from that exercised by Cromwell's religiously biased Commonwealth regime.

Now, political power was once more vested in the hands of the aristocracy. It was hardly dictatorship as Parliament was no longer just an advisory body to the King but a controlling, dynamic organisation which was more than capable of holding the monarch to account.

The House of Lords was immediately re-established and throughout the country there was growing toleration and acceptance of several different Christian doctrines and views. The one denomination that was actively persecuted was Catholicism. The break with Rome was too close, too recent, to allow toleration of any sort.

It was a difficult, dangerous time when the opportunity for anyone to present their beliefs and views was rare. Newspapers were in their infancy, street corner diatribes guaranteed to produce brawling.

A plethora of newly created coffee houses gave what journalist Frank Johnson would later call 'the chattering classes' – in other words the educated middle classes – the opportunity to gather together and debate matters of the day.

Theatres were opened again and, shock of all shocks, women were allowed on the stage to act, dance and sing. In an art form where, prior to Puritan controls, the parts of women were always played by young boys, this was a revolutionary development.

Perhaps more important than any of the other new developments was the behaviour of the young men who were closest in fashion and style, in political and personal views, to the King. The young rakes, as they were known, were almost a clique, determined to make their point and enjoy life. So, too, was the new King Charles: 'The rakes, like the king with his many mistresses, were kicking against the Puritans in society. Their behaviour was calculated to shock and ridicule those who had cut off the head of Charles I.'[3]

It was a clear case of 'come the Restoration, come the emergence of deliberate dissolute behaviour.' What went on was a far cry from the sober, religiously influenced days of the Commonwealth. Encouraged by members of the royal court, groups of drunken young men would now parade up and down the streets at all hours of the day and night.

Outlandish, often highly sexualised, behaviour became almost commonplace. The famous story of one reveller washing his genitalia in a glass of wine before draining the tainted glass in public was soon on the lips of everyone in the city, even if they hadn't seen the actual event.

Such behaviour, viewed from both sides of the religious/political divide, was a knee-jerk reaction by the suddenly emancipated Royalist supporters of Charles, and a clear case of the Puritans standing on their dignity. It was something that led to ill feeling and disgust in the breasts of many of the more sober and Puritanically minded.

At the opposite end of the spectrum from the foppish men-about-town, London could also boast a thriving criminal underworld. In the Whitefriars area of the city, Alsatia as it was then known, existed a sanctuary for thieves and cut throats, criminals of all types and classes. In the narrow streets and alleys of Alsatia these criminals were accepted and protected by householders who readily and easily adhered to the criminal code of never turning in offenders to the authorities, no matter what crime they had committed. When the Great Fire finally erupted, Alsatia was the one community or section of the city that nobody minded seeing consigned to the flames.

Since the days of the first outbreak of bubonic plague in the fourteenth century, the Church had raged against immoral goings on, particularly debauchery and sexual deviancy. There would be recompense, punishment even, the clergy warned. The advent of radical Puritanism had simply made the emotions more tangible and apparent.

Regular church attendance and the purchase of indulgences were intended to reduce the length of time a soul might have to spend in Purgatory but the appeal of immediate pleasure was too great for many of the Royalist faction. At the opposite extreme, the plague and other pandemics during the Middle Ages were, declared the more vitriolic members of the Puritan sects, a sign of heavenly disapproval. Only God's mercy could prevent disaster. But that mercy was hard earned and unless it was looked for immediately, eternal damnation was all that could be expected.

God would exact vengeance: that was a message held and delivered well into the Restoration period by many of the more radical preachers and ministers of the city. The plague was the first sign of God's fury, they declared; the fires of Hell would be next. Expect it soon. After all, according to the Bible, the number of the Beast was 666 and that was far too close to the year 1666 for comfort.

> London must now fall, and who would prevent it? No wonder, when so many pillars are removed, if the building tumbles; the prayers, the tears, and faith which sometimes London hath had, might have quenched the fire, might have opened heaven for rain, and driven back the wind; but now the fire gets the mastery and burns dreadfully, and God with his great bellows blows upon it.[4]

The Reverend Thomas Vincent, who wrote the above lines, went on to declare that what made the Great Fire of London so awful, so much more dismal and depressing than other disasters, was the simple fact that it had begun on the morning of the Lord's Day.

Failure to observe Sunday as a day of rest and worship had long been an issue for 'men of the cloth' and the recent destruction by fire of nearly 600 houses in Oxford and Tiverton, both blazes having occurred on Sundays, was a warning that God was watching, ready to act if he thought it necessary.

During the first few hours of London's Great Fire, before personal fear and concern set in, the comparison to the destruction of Sodom and Gomorrah was an easy label to hang around the necks and shoulders of offenders. God was beginning to punish London and its occupants: that was all people needed to know. That, and the promise of more death and destruction to come:

> God, who hath the winds in his fist, could have gathered in the wind and laid it asleep, or so turned it the other way, that it should have been a defence to the city; or God, who hath the clouds at his command the bottles of heaven in his hand, could have gathered his thick clouds together, and squeezed them; opened his bottles and poured down rain in abundance upon the city. It should have blown water upon the fire which would have quickly blown it out. But the heavens at that time were brass, no showering cloud to be seen.[5]

Despite his rather tortured imagery and the plethora of mixed metaphors in Vincent's somewhat rampant writing style, the message he was trying to send was clear. As surely as he had destroyed Sodom and Gomorrah, God would destroy the city of London and all the people in it if they did not quickly change their ways. You can almost taste the pleasure in Thomas Vincent's words.

* * *

Many had been expecting and fearing a disaster like this for some time. Puritan preachers were particularly adept at prophesying such an event in London, a city that they considered a modern Babylon and the most sinful place on Earth.

Others took a more secular view. They thought of a coming disaster, not perhaps as a punishment for hedonism and debauchery but as a result of conditions in the poorer parts of the city. Failures in the recent wars against the Dutch and the French, along with a decline of profits for the city merchants, were other reasons for predicting trouble ahead.

The recent English Civil War had pitched supporters of Parliament and the King against each other. It had seen thousands on both sides killed or maimed, with property burned or destroyed and, eventually, the King deposed and executed. Had it all been in vain? Rather than admit to that, it was easier and more palatable to fall back on the idea of punishment delivered by a vengeful God.

The early stages of the fire brought panic and confusion. As daylight came on the first Sunday and as the wind grew in ferocity, there was little or no relief. In the minds of many, this was the fiery descent into Hell that the preachers had been promising for years.

It was the wind that really caused most of the damage, pushing the flames westwards, swirling like a typhoon and totally hindering any effects at extinguishing the flames.

Between midnight on Sunday 2 September and dawn on Monday 3rd, effectively the first night of the disaster, the fire grew in strength and magnitude.

Soon, the flames were galloping like a champion racehorse, carving a huge crescent above the city. By midnight on Monday a glowing red semi-circle stretched from Pudding Lane and the Tower of London in the east, heading resolutely towards Cheapside in the west.

To those who stood and watched, it seemed as if both the city and the sky were on fire. Pepys was short but powerful in his description: 'It being darkish, we saw the fire as only one entire arch of fire ¾ an arch of above a mile long. It made me weep to see it.'[6]

Throughout the week leading up to the initial outbreak on 2 September, the wind had increased in ferocity. Even so, nothing prepared the residents of the city for what they witnessed and experienced that first morning.

The diarist John Evelyn, who lived half a dozen miles away in Deptford, first viewed the fire from the south bank of the Thames. Despite himself, he was forced to comment that the seething mass of fire and flame, while spectacular and incredible to view, was both miserable and calamitous. However, from his safe position in Bankside he had, if nothing else, a fine view of proceedings:

> The conflagration was so universal and the people so astonish'd that from the beginning (I know not by what desponding or fate), they hardly stirr'd to quench it, so as there was nothing heard or seene but crying out and lamentations and running about like distracted creatures, without at all attempting to save even their goods; such a strange consternation there was upon them, so it burned in both breadth and length.[7]

Even on the south bank of the Thames, Evelyn could feel the heat from the flames. The screams of the women and children rang in his ears, rising up above 'the cracking and thunder' of the burning buildings.

The copy writers of newspapers like *The London Gazette* were already preparing themselves for future editions of the paper. This was news which, when added to the events of 1665, when the last great visitation of the plague had devastated London, was guaranteed to sell newspapers and preserve the event for posterity.

There was no issue of the *Gazette* for several days after the fire broke out but that delay only served to provide and prepare the reporters and editors with material, much of it hypothetical, some already making judgements about the effects of the Fire: 'It must be observed that the fire happened in a part of town where though the Commodities were not very rich, yet they were so bulky that they could not well be removed so that the Inhabitants of that part where it first began have sustained heavy losses.'[8]

According to *The London Gazette*, people in other parts of the city – the more refined, richer parts in particular – had made better preparations and exit plans for getting themselves and their belongings out of danger. It was elitist, but there was an element of truth in the comment.

Consequently, many of the valuables belonging to the middle classes were saved while those of the workers were burned or stolen. Left in abandoned houses or dumped unceremoniously outside the doors, they were easy targets for opportunist thieves. The comments stoked bad feelings amongst the people, bad feelings that would later come back to the surface.

The newspaper did not stop there, claiming that if the inhabitants had devoted more time and energy to eliminating the fire and less to the saving of their goods, the losses would have been greatly reduced. It was, perhaps, the start of sensationalist journalism?[9]

The sight of Londoners scrabbling for their possessions and taking flight through the city streets impinged itself on the memories of many writers:

> Now fearfulness and terror doth surprise the citizens of London; confusion and astonishment doth fall on them at this unheard of, unthought of, judgement ... now there is a general remove in the city, and that in greater hurry than before the plague, their goods being in greater danger by the fire than the persons were by the sickness.[10]

Goods and possessions were, initially, moved to the houses of friends or relatives. But as the fire spread, those dwellings were also at risk and more movement of valued goods was the inevitable result.

And so, the first day of the disaster came to an end. Even to the uninformed it was clear that things would only get worse, a lot worse, before they could ever begin to look better.

Chapter 2

A Woman Could Piss it Out

The Great Fire of London began shortly before 2.00 a.m. on 2 September 1666. It broke out in the house and business premises of Thomas Farriner, a baker from Pudding Lane.

Pudding Lane was set in a busy part of London, close to the northern end of the famous London Bridge. A short, narrow roadway, the lane was just a few yards distant from Fish Street, which ran parallel to Pudding Lane down to the Thames. Indeed, the two roadways were so close that the rear yards of Farriner's bakery and the Star Inn on Fish Street backed up against each other, with easy access from one set of premises to the next.

The names of the two roads indicate the nature of business in the area. The origin of Fish Street was fairly obvious. Pudding Lane – 'pudding' being the old medieval term for the entrails of cows and sheep – was once the centre of the butchery business in the city. The entrails and other unused parts of the slaughtered beasts were washed down the lane to the river, where they were collected by boats and taken out to sea for dumping. That, at least, was the theory. In reality, much of the waste simply lay in the streets, huge mounds of it stinking and sweating away for weeks on end.

By the middle years of the Stuart era, Pudding Lane, like Fish Street, and other companion roadways, had developed somewhat. Now bakers like Thomas Farriner, cooks, wine sellers and other businessmen had begun to trade out of the narrow lane.

Running downhill towards the river, Fish Street was the main roadway to the Thames and, from there, out over the river via London Bridge. Pudding Lane petered out where it ran into the much larger

Thames Street at the bottom of the hill. Thames Street stretched east and west, parallel to the river, and was lined with massive warehouses, all full of highly toxic and flammable materials.

Farriner, his daughter Hanna, a son also called Thomas, and a servant girl lived above the bakery. They had closed up the shop for the day at the usual time of 9.00 p.m. Saturday, as always, had been busy with housewives and servants from the big houses crowding into Farriner's bakery to purchase pies, bread, pasties, hot ribs of beef and other delicacies.

Farriner's most lucrative business, however, was not with the general public. It lay with the nearby Navy Victualling Office. Farriner produced large quantities of unleavened bread for the sailors on board the ships that were constantly coming and going at the river's many jetties and wharves.

Making the sailors' unleavened bread was a simple enough process but one that needed a firm and steady hand. The bread was baked, thinly sliced and then sold to the Navy as hard tack. Small wonder that Farriner was proud of the appellation 'King's Baker,' an unofficial title which had been bestowed on him and his business by satisfied customers.

After locking up the bakery and shop just after nine, the baker and his daughter had gone back downstairs at about midnight. Farriner was trying to find a light for his candle while Hanna began making a final check of the oven and other dead or dying fires in the house.

The huge, oval oven, made in the popular beehive style, stood in Farriner's yard. It was made from bricks and was lit by putting a match to bunches of kindling on its floor. Careful management of the oven was required as sparks could easily leap from the kindling onto other flammable materials stored in the yard.

Now, when Hanna checked it, the faggots of wood and the remains of the kindling had been raked out. The oven was cold and closed up. Having obtained a light for his candle from one of the downstairs fire grates, Farriner retired once more to his room. There was, it seemed, nothing to concern him or any of the shop employees.

Farriner was wrong. Somehow – and no-one has ever really come up with an unquestionable explanation – not long after the baker had retired to bed, a spark leapt out from the supposedly dead oven and landed on a pile of kindling. The wind and the dry wood did the rest.

The occupants of the house were asleep in their beds when Farriner's male assistant, who slept in a room located downstairs, woke with a choking cough. He smelled what he thought was burning. Pulling himself to his feet, the man saw clouds of dense smoke rolling towards him. Behind them, he glimpsed the orange-red glow of flames. The building was alight and, by the looks of things, the fire was already out of control.

The assistant baker managed to battle his way through the smoke and climb the stairs to Farriner's quarters. The baker was quickly alerted of the danger but when he, his son, daughter, and other household staff tried to get down the stairway, they were beaten back by the flames and the heat. The only option now was to attempt an escape over the roof.

Crawling out of a garret window, Thomas Farriner led the way along the guttering towards the house next door, where they hoped to be welcomed and admitted to safety. The route across the slippery guttering might promise safety but it was a difficult and dangerous journey.

One slip and somebody, perhaps everyone in the party, would be looking at a drop of 30 or 40 feet onto the cobbles below. Nobody dared to look down. The servant girl, in particular, was terrified of heights and the thought of the drop. She convinced herself that she would fall and so turned back to the burning building.

There was little attempt to persuade the servant girl to stay on the roof with the escapees. Saving their own skin was the aim of all Farriner's party. They managed to escape the flames but for the servant girl the inevitable soon happened. Back in the bakery, she was overcome by the smoke and acrid air and suffocated to death. Her name remains unknown, but she was the first fatality in the Great Fire of London.

Farriner and his group cried out warnings and alarms as they went over the roof and soon their calls were mirrored from below. The shout of 'Fire!' was quickly repeated from the lane and from nearby streets.

Soon a crowd began to gather as people were roused from their beds and came outside their houses to discover the cause of the alarm.

In an age of literary magnificence, the poet Samuel Wiseman may not have been a great versifier but he caught the mood of the moment in the first four lines of his poem on the fire, the title of which – *A Short and serious narrative of London's fatal fire with its diurnal and nocturnal progressing from Sunday morning (being the second of September) to the Wednesday night following* – was almost as long as the poem itself:

> And now the doleful, dreadful, hideous Note
> Of Fire is screamed out with a deep strained throat;
> Horror and fear, and sad distracted cries
> Chide sloth away, and bid the sluggards rise[1]

Sluggards or not, the vast majority of the crowd staring at Farriner's burning bakery were not helpers or firefighters but just interested onlookers. This was entertainment, free entertainment, and the mood of the people was relatively happy. For the moment at least, they and their properties were safe. The bakery might burn; let it smoulder, as long as their shops and houses were safe.

Realising that Farriner's property was close to destruction, most of the spectators soon moved to the rear yard of the Star Inn on Fish Street. With the yards of the Star and Farriner's bakery backing onto each other, it was relatively safe there and the view of the burning bakery was just as good. Or so they thought.

For an hour it seemed as if the blaze had been contained to Farriner's bakery and house. The parish constables, alerted to the problem, soon arrived and thought differently. This was a potentially major fire, and Sir Thomas Bludworth, the Lord Mayor, ought to be informed. This was duly done and Bludworth, muttering oaths and regrets over his disturbed night's sleep, soon arrived in Pudding Lane. What he saw there immediately terrified him.

Contrary to public opinion, most of which was just wishful thinking, the fire had not been contained; it was already creeping down Pudding

Lane and Fish Street, moving inexorably towards the waiting warehouses of Thames Street. If those storage depots caught fire the result would be catastrophic. Bludworth stood open-mouthed, not knowing what he should do.

Almost immediately, more practical and realistic citizens advised Bludworth that the fire had already spread too far and too quickly for water to be of much use, even if decent supplies could be found. The only way of stopping the fire now was by pulling down houses ahead of the advancing flames to create fire breaks.

Whatever limited courage and ability Bludworth possessed immediately disappeared. He had neither the authority nor the intention of pulling down any houses: 'Bludworth simply said that he dared not do it without the consent of the owners. Most of the shops and homes were rented so that those owners were God knows where. Not in Pudding Lane for sure.'[2]

Bludworth did have something of a point. Homeowners had the right to sue for compensation or the cost of rebuilding any properties pulled down to stop a fire. As Lord Mayor, Bludworth did actually have the authority to destroy houses and create fire breaks but that simply made him, as chief representative of the city, responsible for the destruction. Financial ruin hovered over the shoulders of the terrified Thomas Bludworth.

Despite the strength of the wind and flames, Bludworth was reluctant to change his mind. The fire was not that serious, he declared. And anyway, if houses were pulled down, who was going to pay for replacements? Certainly not him.

With that he shrugged and made his infamous remark which has gone down in history and legend – 'A woman might piss it out.' He turned on his heel and went home. He was, he said, tired from lack of sleep and from dealing with men who would simply not obey his instructions. The firefighters were probably better off without him.

* * *

With Bludworth virtually abdicating his responsibility, control passed to the leading citizens of the area. They were as helpless as the Lord Mayor and were also just as reticent in dealing with the burning buildings and shops. Their efforts during the remainder of the night were mainly attempts at containment, extinguishing what was already there in front of their eyes rather than preventing the fire's further progress. It was hard and difficult work, almost impossible in many cases.

Many of the leather buckets that were supposed to carry water from the Thames to the fires had ruptured and split from lack of maintenance. There was little option but to use household items like jugs and kettles. With these simple articles pressed into emergency use, it was obvious that the citizens were fighting a losing battle.

Suddenly, as the watchers in the yard of the Star Inn looked excitedly on, there was a roar and the roof of Thomas Farriner's house and bakery collapsed. The walls fell inwards and sparks, pieces of paper, balks of timber and hunks of burning wood were flung into the air. There they were caught by the wind and blown wildly about the streets. Soon, the detritus of the collapsed building was igniting fires several streets away. The Star Inn was one of the first to explode into fire and flames.

The crowd in the yard of the Star Inn immediately dispersed and fled to their own houses. Many of these were already burning but those that were still intact were soon the scene of drastic and dramatic action.

This time, the sudden spate of activity was fuelled by panic. All goods and possessions of value were carried outside by the householders, some tied up in bundles, others simply carried on men's shoulders. They were well advised to clear out as much as possible from their houses as the advance of the flames was inexorable.

For the rest of the night the citizens of London tried their hardest to control the blaze. The fire, however, was relentless and moved faster than anyone had thought possible. In a matter of minutes the flames spread from house to house, from street to street. By dawn the whole of Fish Street, the main thoroughfare down to the river, was ablaze.

The sky above London glowed red and orange, the roar of the flames and the screams of terrified people deafening to all who heard them:

> The noise and cracking and thunder of the impetuous flames, the shrieking of women and children, the hurry of people, the fall of towers, houses and churches was like some hideous storm and the air all about so hot and inflamed that at the last one was not able to approach it, so that they were forced to stand still and let the flames burn on.[3]

News of the fire spread almost as quickly as the flames. The sudden destruction of St Magnus the Martyr church, flames leaping up its spire and bringing down the tall belfry, alerted many of the more distant citizens. A mixture of excitement and terror filled the air.

Sir Thomas Bludworth, in his final few months as the Lord Mayor, returned to Pudding Lane and Fish Street soon after daybreak. His conscience was clearly troubling him, but on arriving back at the original seat of the fire, it was clear that his attitude remained the same. Despite what he could see in front of him he still believed that this was no more than a minor fire that would soon burn itself out.

Yet again, he was advised to pull down a number of houses and create fire breaks. If he had agreed to this earlier in the night, it might well have worked. Now the fire was too far advanced, moving quicker than men could destroy even the flimsiest of buildings.

The destruction of private property would probably not have made an awful lot of difference and it was, anyway, a rhetorical question. Bludworth refused and kept refusing to pull down any houses, asking simply who was going to pay the owners for the damage and then shoulder the cost of rebuilding.

Debate was, as Bludworth well knew, immaterial. He was not going to start pulling down privately owned property and really did not care who paid out compensation. It was not going to be him. Stopping the fire before it destroyed the entire city should have been his chief aim. Instead, he was far more concerned with protecting his own back.

In their defence, Bludworth and the others had little or no idea about the identity of the house owners. They could have found out but it would have taken time. What was required was a rapid and dynamic response. It needed brave decisions and rapid action in the face of awful danger. What the city of London got that day was indecision.

In hindsight and with time to consider the actions of their Lord Mayor, many people blamed Bludworth for the disaster. He should have acted sooner was the general consensus – a surprisingly mild rebuke considering that he had not acted at all!

John Evelyn was one of the few people to defend Thomas Bludworth. Without giving figures or names, he wrote in his diary that many of the 'gentlemen' advising the King roused themselves from inactivity to put forward the idea that only one action was likely to save the city – blowing up houses in large numbers.

Destruction of property and creating larger than normal fire breaks was not an original idea. It had been done before, both in London and in other cities and towns where serious fires had broken out.

Sailors from nearby ships, either docked at one of London's many quays or lying out in midstream, had been advocating the use of explosives for some hours. It was quicker than the traditional method of hooking and pulling at burning walls, but explosives needed careful, expert handling. The presence of the sailors would have provided exactly that but the idea was dismissed out of hand.

Once again without giving names, Evelyn chose to put the blame for refusal to follow their advice on anonymous members of the gentry and local councils, people other than Thomas Bludworth:

> Nothing was like to put a stop but the blowing up of so many houses, as might make a wider gap than any that had yet been made by the ordinary method of pulling them downe with engines. This some stout seamen proposed early enough to have saved the

> whole City; but some tenacious and avaricious Men, Aldermen etc, would not permit it because their houses must have been of the first.[4]

While debate raged, so too did the fire. Shortly after dawn on Sunday the blaze had worked its way down Fish Street and Pudding Lane to reach Thames Street at the foot of the hill. Within minutes most of the warehouses and storage yards along the riverbank were on fire. Nearby London Bridge and the houses that lined it were now under serious risk of destruction.

* * *

Early on that fateful Sunday morning there came a brief respite. A sudden and short-lived drop in the wind halted the fire's progress to the west. A united sigh of relief was broken by the realisation that the wind, relentless to the last, had not died but simply changed direction. It was now blowing the fire eastwards towards the older part of the city. More houses and St Botolph's church in the Billingsgate area joined the church of St Magnus the Martyr as burnt-out ruins.

Even more worrying was the sudden realisation that the fire might now reach the Tower of London. In the Tower lay huge quantities of gunpowder, stored there for the protection of the city. If the fire should reach the most powerful citadel in the country, the result would be catastrophic.

The panic was cut short when, by luck rather than design, the wind picked up again. Once again it came powering in from the east and the fire's westward march resumed.

By now people were wandering, even running, mindlessly along the city streets, most of them in utter confusion. It was not just the fire that lay behind the chaos. The fear of a foreign attack on the city was once more rampant, as it had been all summer. Only now, in the minds of many, there was proof positive that the enemy had come.

War against the United Provinces had been raging for two years, the Dutch finding an ally in the powerful nation of France in January 1666. Faced by this powerful alliance, the British navy had fought several actions, notably a victory by General Monck over the Dutch fleet in August, barely three weeks before the Great Fire.

Most of the altercations between the three nations had been inconclusive, although the French capture of St Kitts in the West Indies had been a bitter blow. There were compensations, however.

A landing by British troops on Vlie and Schelling islands saw over 150 Dutch trading vessels destroyed and the town of Brandaris put to the sword. Fire had destroyed many of the buildings, a point not lost on Londoners.

Surprisingly, Monck's successes had not given the inhabitants of London the confidence and pride that might have been expected. Throughout the long, hot summer fear was rampant, everyone expecting the Dutch and French to retaliate for the humiliation of their naval defeat. A fire for a fire: this one was, many believed, the first act of revenge on the part of their enemies.

As the September Sunday night was succeeded by day, the fear that had consumed the city coalesced into violence. Anger had been simmering and now, in some cases, it exploded.

William Taswell, then a young scholar at Westminster School, wrote that the crowds – 'the ignorant and deluded mob,' as he called them – went searching for Catholics and Frenchmen. In their eyes the two groups were exactly the same:

> A blacksmith in my presence, meeting an innocent Frenchman walking along the street, felled him instantly to the ground with an iron bar … In another place I saw the incensed population divesting a French printer of all the goods in his shop, and after helping him off with many other things, levelling his house to the ground.[5]

The reason for destroying the Frenchman's house? People thought he was about to add to the conflagration by setting his own property alight, thus extending the scope of the Great Fire. Why someone should destroy his own house and livelihood was never considered. There were many more mistakes and misunderstandings that morning, emotion overtaking all rational thought.

Incident rapidly followed incident as the London mob began to flex its unified muscles. One Frenchman who had made his home in the city was attacked and nearly killed by a crowd of workmen because he was thought to be carrying a box full of incendiary grenades. They were tennis balls.

Another man, English to the bone, was apprehended and flung into prison simply because he looked like a Frenchman. As many of the unfortunates had been assaulted and attacked, prison was a safer bet than being on the streets.

It was said that 4,000 French and Dutch invaders had landed and were now getting ready to advance into the city. Some rumourmongers put the total of enemy soldiers as high as 12,000. Of course, none of them ever appeared, but many Londoners found security in collecting sticks, cudgels and axes, and gathering themselves into a 'people's army.' They could and should have been engaged in fighting the fire, not imaginary Frenchmen. And so the fire raged on.

Despite the clear presence of fire, the fears and concerns of London's citizens were mostly intangible and centred on the issue of trade. London depended on trade; it had grown and prospered on the back of merchant ships taking and receiving goods to and from countries across the world.

Such a process was financially rewarding but in time of war it was also highly vulnerable. Now, in what was effectively a commercial war, the Dutch had persuaded the combined Scandinavian countries to close the route from the North Sea into the Baltic to all British shipping.

That embargo undoubtedly hurt London's trade but the Dutch had then taken the matter a stage further by employing privateers to destroy

British merchants' ships. By the summer of 1666 it was calculated that over 300 British merchant vessels had been sunk and captured. Small wonder, then, that this fire was viewed not as an accident but as yet another example of Dutch infamy.

John Evelyn wrote sympathetically but honestly about the extent of the fire on this Sunday morning, showing the damage it had done during the night:

> The fire having continued all this night (if I may call that night, which was as light as day for 10 miles around about after a dreadful manner) when conspiring with a fierce Easterly Wind in a very drie season ... I saw the whole south part of the cittie [sic] burning from Cheapside to the Thames and all along Cornhill ... O, the miserable and calamitous spectacle, such as happily the whole world has not seen the like since the foundation of it.[6]

As London burned and Thomas Bludworth pontificated, ordinary men and women sought to rescue what they could from the flames. For the first time since the fire began, private goods and possessions were to be seen floating in the Thames. It was a sight that both John Evelyn and Samuel Pepys would write about in the days ahead.

The tragedy of that first night was Bludworth's failure to act. Even on his second visit to Pudding Lane and its environs, this time in daylight, there was still a possibility that he might save the day and become the hero of the hour. Had he ordered the pulling down of houses it still might – and the significant word is 'might' – have made a difference.

If and might – two significant words that early autumn day. If Bludworth had gathered his wits and thought not of the existing fires but of what was waiting ahead, it might have led to a different outcome. By looking ahead for the answer, it would not have been too difficult to see that working in advance of the fire might offer a degree of salvation.

If fire breaks had been created in the hours before the blaze actually reached them, that might have stopped the fire in its tracks. That would almost certainly have been the case if they had been twice as long or wide as the normal breaks. The key would have been to break the passage of hot air and abnormally high temperatures, 'flashover' as it was known, from one house to the next.

Much of the involvement of Lord Mayor Thomas Bludworth remains lodged in the realm of 'What if?' Like most rhetorical questions, it is fascinating but not really productive. We will never know what might have happened if Bludworth had finally got his act together.

Chapter 3

A View From the Window

Samuel Pepys and his wife Elizabeth had spent the Saturday evening at the playhouse. After the performance they dined in Islington where, in his own words, they 'ate, drank and made mighty merry.' As midnight approached they went home in their carriage, singing as they went. When they reached their house Elizabeth Pepys immediately took herself to bed while Samuel wrote a few letters for the Admiralty before joining his wife in their bedroom.

Pepys had been provided with his house in Seething Lane as an integral part of his salary as Clerk of the Acts to the Navy Board. Part office, part home, it was barely a quarter of a mile from the seat of the fire. It meant that, should he want it, Samuel Pepys had a great view of events. However, to begin with he was not impressed:

> Some of our maids sitting up late last night to get things ready against our feast today, Jane called us up, about 3.00 in the morning to tell us of a great fire they saw in the city. So I rose, and slipped on my nightgown and went to her window … I thought it far enough off, and so went to bed again and to sleep.[1]

He woke at about 7.00 and decided to take another look at the fire. It seemed smaller than before and further away. Then Jane, his servant girl, arrived to inform Pepys that the fire had already claimed upwards of 300 houses and that it was now burning its way down Fish Street towards London Bridge. Pepys remained sceptical.

Somewhat reluctantly, however, he dressed and decided to take a closer look. He walked towards the Tower of London, where he met the Lieutenant of the Tower, Sir John Robinson.

Pepys had little time for Robinson, considering him something of a buffoon, but the Lieutenant told him how the fire had started in Pudding Lane at about 2.00 a.m. It had, Robinson informed him in stentorian tones, already destroyed the Church of St Magnus and many of the houses in Fish Street and Pudding Lane.

Never one to rely on second-hand information, Pepys decided to see the extent of the blaze for himself. Accompanied by Robinson's small son, he climbed to the top of one of the towers and there he witnessed the full progress of the fire. The houses on London Bridge were already in flames and wherever he looked he saw people running for their lives. Climbing back down, Pepys exchanged a few words with Robinson and thought he should take an even closer look: 'So I down to the water-side and there got a boat and through the bridge, and there saw the lamentable fire ... It got as far as Stillyard while I was there. Everybody [was] endeavouring to remove their goods, and flinging them into the river or bringing them into lighters that lay off.'[2]

Lightermen and boatmen realised that the fire had given them a great opportunity to make money out of the disaster. Boats were available for those who wanted to move goods to safety, perhaps to the dwelling of a friend or relative, or even to escape themselves but they made it abundantly clear that it was going to cost the terrified Londoners dearly.

With the normal rate of boat hire being approximately £5, the boat owners now decided that demand and danger warranted an increase in fees. Human nature being what it is, some boatmen were charging as much as £30 for a few hours' hire.

As the day progressed more and more Londoners decided that simply moving goods and possessions from one house to another was a pointless exercise as the fire was moving quickly and the whole procedure would soon have to be repeated within a few hours. It was time to flee the city.

If there were no boats available, there were always carters or waggoners who would happily fill their vehicles with paying customers along with their valuable possessions. Then they would give their horses their heads and get out of the city. From there it was simple – a quick trip to a nearby park or piece of open ground, drop off the cargo and then head back into the streets of London for another load! It was an easy and profitable process, in theory at least.

It was not just London-based waggoners who filled their carts – and their pockets – with the prized possessions of the panic-stricken Londoners, along with the money they had initially paid to keep them safe. As news of the fire spread across the city walls and out into the countryside, wagons poured out from those surrounding rural areas into the city streets.

If the boatmen had been first in the queue, the carters and waggoners proved to be experts in the business of fleecing their customers:

> Now, carts and drays, and coaches, and horses, as many as could have entrance to the city, were loaded, and any money was given for help; five, ten, twenty, and thirty pounds for a cart to bear forth into the fields some choice things, which were ready to be consumed; and some of the countries had the conscience to accept of the highest price which the citizens did offer in their extremity.[3]

The narrowness of the roads and lanes, combined with the excessive number of heavily laden carts, made escape from the city a difficult, not to say dangerous occupation. Piled high with goods, taking corners was a problem for the eager waggoners and many valuable goods, valuable to the owners, at least, were lost over the sides to lie in the gutters until they were purloined by street urchins.

Carts, cabs and wagons sometimes found themselves stuck for hours in traffic jams of ever- increasing proportions. And that, of course, gave thieves and pilferers from the darker regions of the city the chance to exploit their art to the full. Suffice to say, crime was rampant, both during the course of the fire and in the immediate post-fire period.

The emphasis of the authorities lay on rebuilding and repairing city life. Thieving and pilfering were way down the list of priorities.

Theft was probably the most common crime during this intense but relatively short period. Plundering and looting became common practice. These were opportunist crimes, however, not always committed by hardened criminals but often by ordinary citizens who saw their lives and livelihood disappearing before their eyes.

With very little policing of the streets, the chance to steal food, clothing and money seemed to be too good a chance to miss. The professional thieves simply carried on with their jobs, happy to exploit the situation while it lasted.

In Stuart London the theft of anything valued above a shilling was usually met by capital punishment but, with the fire raging, need overcame demands for justice. There was little to be gained from hanging men and women of previously good character. In any case, it would have taken months, maybe years, to arrest and prosecute all the offenders. The courts would simply be blocked. Consequently, a decision was taken to waive punishment as long as the plundered goods were returned to their rightful owners. It was a necessary decision to offer an amnesty but what it also offered was a thieves' paradise.

Stealing from the back of the wagons was simple enough, especially if the vehicles were stuck in ever-increasing traffic. Easier still was the opportunity to loot abandoned houses. The owners might have removed what they considered their prized possessions but would have been forced to leave much behind. To the plunderers, anything left in the abandoned houses was fair game.

The really clever thieves were the ones who would collect a fee, load their wagons and then disappear into the distance before the owners realised what was happening. Fortunately, the density of the traffic and the deadlock it created made this particular criminal activity a fairly short-lived problem.

Information about the fate of looters and plunderers is limited, either because they got away with their crimes or because they took advantage of the amnesty offered by the local councils and parishes.

The unfortunate Mary Fisher was one who did not get away with it, at least in the beginning. Accused of stealing several large quantities of Virginia tobacco from a dealer by the name of John Martin, she was sent to appear before the Middlesex Sessions at the end of September 1666.[4]

What eventually became of her is unknown as, after the documentation detailing her referral to the Middlesex Sessions, she disappeared from view again. The legal system, normally punitive in the extreme, was in the process of offering largesse and goodwill to as many petty criminals as possible. It is, therefore, entirely probable that Mary Fisher, like so many others, benefitted from the short but effective amnesty.

By mid-afternoon on the first Sunday of the fire, the swirling flames had been driven first one way, then another. The fire had now leapt onto the first houses on the northern side of London Bridge.

What could have been a disaster, however, was averted by sheer luck. A large space in the lines of buildings along the bridge acted as a fire break and the flames could not get past. The bridge survived, although fire damage meant that it could not be used as an escape route.

Flying debris had caused an outbreak of fire on the southern side of the river but prompt action by the residents had managed to contain it. The northern bank was not nearly so fortunate. As the wind shifted the flames moved inexorably in a north-westerly direction. For the fleeing residents of the city, it was now a case of boat, horse and cart or nothing.

* * *

London Bridge and its houses might have been saved but for so many other parts of the city destruction and disaster still loomed.

Thames Street ran along the margin of the river, creating a barrier to the south of the fire. Along the length of the street stood vulnerable and valuable warehouses, most of them containing vast quantities of tar, oil and other flammable materials. Unofficial bands of 'watchers and fighters' had been formed to monitor the fire along the street.

Watchers were particularly needed as rumour and threats of explosive bombs or grenades thrown by foreigners were still there: 'Trained bands are up in arms, watching at every quarter for outlandish men, because of the general fears and jealousies, and rumours that fireballs were thrown into houses by several of them, to help on and provoke the too furious flames.'[5]

What many of the watchers were now witnessing was a curious and highly dangerous phenomenon where oxygen in the wind caused sudden and unpredictable explosions that were virtually impossible to fight. In the world of pyrotechnics, it is a process that is still known as flashover.

Flashover was the ignition, without obvious warning, of combustible items in a house, warehouse or any enclosed space. It normally occurred when the temperature in a burning room exceeded 1,100 degrees Fahrenheit, causing thermal decomposition of material and items and the release of flammable gases.[6]

In 1666 flashover was recognised as a possibility in any serious outbreak of fire, but its cause was not understood. Nobody could conceive of any reason why sudden intense heat and accompanying explosions should rampage through the city, ahead of the flames. And yet it was happening, there before their eyes.

What made this example of flashover during the Great Fire so unusual, however, was that it was not just happening in the houses and shops but also in the streets of London. It was a terrifying experience, even for men well-schooled and experienced in the art of firefighting. People could be working on a burning house when, suddenly, three or four houses ahead of them, another building would erupt in flames.

There had been no sign of fire, no passage of flame, just intense heat and clouds or layers of dense smoke. Occasionally flashover would be accompanied by tongues of flame but these were simply interpreted as the progress of the fire. The most terrifying aspect of flashover was that there was no fire to be seen, just intense heat to be felt and then an explosion of flame and smoke.

In any enclosed space the layers of smoke would spread up to the ceiling before exploding. In London's streets there were no ceilings but there were dozens upon dozens of jettied houses almost touching each other and creating what was virtually a roof over the roads and alleyways. There were obvious gaps in these 'ceilings' but the covering was enough to spark flashover.

The unexpected explosions and outbreaks of fire when everything was seemingly under control were mystifying. But to the people of London there was one obvious cause. Foreign agents, in the pay of Dutch and French terrorists, were throwing fire bombs through the windows of buildings and adding to the carnage. It added to the terror and the fear that flashover – in the guise of the Dutch or French – could happen anywhere.

* * *

We left Samuel Pepys in a boat on the river. After an hour he decided that there was nothing more he could see, do or discover. He had seen the panic of the people in the streets and on the Thames, noticing in particular that virtually nobody was attempting to quench the fire but trying to save their own goods and lives.

He had been active all morning, being rowed through the arches of London Bridge to record the length and strength of the fire. He had discovered that the great waterwheels beneath the bridge, wheels that should have pumped out water to fight the fire, had been destroyed by the very enemy they had been meant to eliminate.

There was little more he could do. However, he paused long enough to watch the demise of the pigeons which had, for years, annoyed and troubled the residents and visitors. Tongue in cheek, Pepys got his revenge for the pigeon droppings on his windowsills and coat tails: 'And among other things, the poor pigeons I perceive were loath to leave their houses, but hovered about the windows and balconies till they were some of them burned, their wings, and fell down.'[7]

After that, Pepys directed his boatman to pull hard for Whitehall. He had not forgotten his duties as a civil servant and guessed that the King, and the members of his court, would want to know the latest details. He was not far wrong.

Disembarking and making his way towards the King's Closet in the chapel, Pepys was immediately surrounded by dozens of courtiers and officials, all desperate to know what was happening. Pulled and prodded, he still managed to paint a lurid but accurate picture, so much so that King Charles immediately summoned him into his presence for a more private report.

Pepys did not pull his punches. He was virulent about the lack of action from Sir Thomas Bludworth and the inevitability of total destruction unless something was done:

> I was called for and did tell the King and the Duke of York what I saw, and that unless His Majesty did command houses to be pulled down, nothing could stop the fire. They seemed much troubled and the King commanded me to go to my Lord Mayor from him and command him to spare no houses but to pull down before the fire every way.[8]

Before he left Whitehall to return to the city, James, Duke of York, ordered Pepys to promise the Lord Mayor more soldiers if he needed them. Large numbers of the King's Guard had already been sent into the city to lend their hands in extinguishing the blaze and James's offer to send even more men was quite genuine.

Pepys, like many others, was wary of too many soldiers being present in the confines of a London still on edge as far as Royalist supporters were concerned. For the moment, at least, he decided to keep the offer to himself.

He was given the use of a royal carriage and was hurriedly sent off to London. At first all went well, but somewhere near St Paul's Cathedral the crowded streets became impassable and Pepys was forced to abandon the coach and walk the rest of the way into the city. Going against the press of the crowd was not easy but eventually he managed to make his way into Cannon Street. His great dilemma now was where to find Bludworth.

Fortunately, he found the Lord Mayor in Cannon Street, accompanied by one or two assistants. He looked, Pepys later wrote, like a man who has spent all his energy and determination and was now wandering helplessly through his domain. When Pepys gave him the King's message the shock was clearly visible to everyone: 'To the King's message he cried like a fainting woman "Lord! What can I do? I am spent: people will not obey me. I have been pulling down houses, but the fire overtakes us faster than we can do it."'[9]

With that he informed Pepys that he had been up all night and needed rest and food. He turned and went home. Pepys was astounded by the lies and by Bludworth's attitude but he knew he could do very little. So, remembering the 'feast' he was supposed to be giving that day, he followed the Lord Mayor's example and walked home for lunch.

That afternoon, without direction or support from the Mayor, the more astute citizens began moving their possessions from their own houses and storing them with friends. They did not realise that they would soon have to move them on again.

Some of them were resorting to more dramatic actions, starting to pull down houses to create fire breaks. Their efforts were uncoordinated, however, and therefore, relatively ineffective. The citizens needed to be directed but order and control were the very last things they were offered.

Pepys and his guests, all of whom had turned up for the feast, regardless of the fire, apparently enjoyed an excellent meal. Then Pepys and one of his guests, a man by the name of Mr Moone, took a walk through the burning city. It was the same old story: men and women trying their best but in effect getting almost nowhere.

Pepys and Moone parted at St Paul's Cathedral, little knowing that the massive church would soon be smouldering like the rest of the city.

Pepys went to the Thames and claimed yet another boat. The oarsman pulled quickly away from the moorings before the tiny vessel could be overwhelmed by fleeing citizens. On the river, Pepys met King Charles and his brother James. Pulling their barge close alongside Pepys's vessel, the King repeated his instructions to pull down more houses and create fire breaks.

Leaving the royal brothers to their own devices, Pepys met his wife, as arranged, in St James' Park. She was accompanied by two friends. The four eager watchers took to the water again, staring at the fires and trying to gauge the progress of the flames:

> All over the Thames, with one's face in the wind you were almost burned with a shower of Firedrops so as houses were burned by these drops and flakes of fire, three or four, nay five and six houses, one from another. When we could endure no more upon the water, we to a little alehouse on the Bankside over against the Three Cranes, and there stayed till it was dark and saw the fire grow.[10]

It is understandable that Pepys should allocate blame for the fire spreading, leaping five or six houses at one go, to what he called firedrops. In many cases the firedrops were partly to blame for the quick spread of the fire. Firedrops and flashover? The combination was deadly.

Reading the diary entries of Samuel Pepys for this period, there is a clear bias or leaning towards travel writing, modern travel writing where the author is central to everything that happens, everything he sees. How the events and the environment affect him is crucial to the article – or, in this case, to the diary entry.

Pepys seems to have enjoyed walking through the burning city, occasionally bemoaning the fate of the buildings and of their inhabitants. The key to the success of his writing lies in his ability to retain that personal involvement, recording what happened to him, how it made him feel and so on. He describes and details the destruction of the city but never actually divorces himself from what is going on.

You cannot help feeling that the writer in Pepys is actually enjoying the fire. His work, his finished product, is therefore very different from the work of men like Vincent and Evelyn.

Vincent, always conscious of God's involvement, felt able to comment on the emotional state of the Londoners. His, however, is a distant, third-person view of the disaster: 'Now hopes begin to sink. And a general consternation seizeth on the spirits of the people; little sleep is taken in London this night.'[11]

The modern reader understands how the inhabitants of the city are feeling and how their past behaviour has influenced divine judgement but Vincent remains the external, impartial observer.

John Evelyn, inevitably the possessor of a more poetic turn than the Reverend Vincent, described one of his visits to the city in more personal tones, passing on an accurate but disturbing picture of what he had seen and felt. He is still somewhat distant from events: 'With extraordinary difficulty, clambering over mountaines [sic] of yet smouldering rubbish, and frequently mistaking where I was, the ground under my feet so hot as made me not only Sweate [sic], but even burnt the soles of my shoes.'[12]

Pepys, on the other hand, wrote time and again about his walks through the burning city, recording things like his boat hire and the people he met and helped: 'At night lay down a little upon a quilt of W. Hewer in the office (all of my own things being packed up or gone) and after me my poor wife did the like – we having fed upon the remains of yesterday's dinner, having no fire nor dishes, nor any opportunity of dressing anything.'[13]

All three writers contributed to the record and descriptions of the Great Fire of London. But Samuel Pepys, with his account of how the blaze actually affected him, remains the one man whose work we cannot do without.

Of course, there were other people who wrote about the disaster, men like the Reverend Thomas Vincent and the schoolboy William Taswell, even a Spanish visitor who later published his account in one of the Spanish newspapers. Poets and writers like John Dryden were active, even though most of them wrote with the benefit of time and leisure between them and the fire.

In his *Annus Mirabilis*, the poet John Dryden took the tragedy of the now homeless Londoners and painted a graphic but tragic view of the displaced people:

> Those who have homes, when homes they do repair
> To a last lodging call their wandering friends.
> Their short uneasy sleeps are broke with care,
> To look how near their own destruction tends:
> Those who have none sit round where once it was.
> And with full eyes each wonted room require,
> Haunting the yet warm ashes of the place,
> As murdered men walk where they did expire.[14]

Splendid and descriptive as Dryden's poem might be, it was still something produced with hindsight, long after any danger had passed. For graphic and powerful poetry and prose, written in fear and laden with the sense of doom that hung in the air above the city and the smoke, we turn to people like Samuel Pepys and John Evelyn.

Chapter 4

Day Two: The King, the Duke and Samuel Pepys

Sunday, the first day of the Great Fire of London, eventually came to an end with smoke and flames enveloping large quantities of the city's houses. To the north, to the west, and even to the east, buildings groaned, shook and collapsed in showers of sparks and fire. By nightfall the flames had already spread for 1,600 feet along the banks of the Thames. There seemed to be no way of extinguishing the flames.

With the fire growing progressively fiercer and more destructive, even Samuel Pepys was at last forced to consider his position. Shortly after midnight he accepted the fact that his house could well burn – although, as it happened, it didn't – and so the careful Pepys took suitable precautions. His descriptions were unlike most of his previous writings. The sentences were convoluted and sometimes ungrammatical, showing the stress he was labouring under: 'And did by Moonshine (it being brave, dry, and moonshine and warm weather) carry much of my goods into the garden, and Mr Hater and I did remove my money and Iron Chests into my cellar – as thinking that the safest place. And got my bags of gold into my office ready to carry away.'[1]

Pepys did not go to bed that Sunday night, busying himself about the office and the house. About 4.00 on Monday morning he was disturbed by a waggoner hammering on the door. The man had been sent by Pepys's patron and friend Lady Batten. She had despatched the cart to carry away to safety all of Pepys's valuable possessions, money included.

The ever-wary Pepys was relieved and happy with the gift from Lady Batten but he still went with the cart to ensure it remained safe from the hands of pilferers and thieves and was able to reach its destination. He rode on the back of the wagon dressed in his nightgown.

The streets were still crowded, even at that time of the morning, with men and women pushing, shoving and shouldering their way towards safety. There were even sick people who were being carried or wheeled in their beds through the streets in an effort to take them out of danger. And all the time, the roaring of the flames echoed like wild beasts in everyone's ears.

By evening Samuel Pepys was back in Seething Lane. He was soon helping his wife Elizabeth to load the more cumbersome items of furniture onto a rowing boat or lighter at Tower Dock. He was lucky to find one available. The boat and its contents were taken to the home of George Carteret in Deptford.

John Evelyn was quick to comment on the sounds of the burning city. Much of it, he noted, was coming from the crowds of people who were shocked and confused by the severity of the fire. So great was their distress, he wrote, that their wailing and crying almost wiped out the roar of the flames – almost, but not quite: 'Nothing heard but crying out and lamentations … [then came] the fall of towers, houses and churches, like an [sic] hideous storme and the aire all about so hot and inflam'd that at the last one was not able to approach it.'[2]

Like Pepys and so many others who were later to write their accounts, Evelyn had noted the fire leaping in what he termed 'a prodigious manner from house to house and street to street, at great distances from each other.' But like his colleagues, he had no idea what was causing the strange phenomenon or how to cure it. The cure, when it finally came, was a modern development but that was many years in the future.

Having secured his goods with friends, Samuel Pepys returned to his own house, endangered as it was. There was, he noted, a subtle change in the atmosphere, not in the environment but in the attitude of the people.

As morning dawned on Monday 3 September, a revitalised sense of order and control seemed to have been brought with it.

People appeared to be saying to themselves that they had survived the night and now it was time to do something about the devastation caused by the fire. It was an attitude that showed the strength of the Londoners, their resilience rather than the panic of the day before. Even so, it did not stop the spread of the fire.

Despite the changing attitude of the people, the city continued to burn, pushing relentlessly north and west. It was a terrifying sight, flames leaping dramatically from one property to the next, one warehouse to its nearest neighbour. The difference, for now at least, seemed to be a desire in the populace to extinguish the flames.

What was needed, however, was a leader to take control of the situation and exploit the new-found courage of the people. King Charles had the answer to that particular conundrum.

At the request of the King, the Duke of York now assumed command of the firefighting operations. The King would probably have preferred to take complete control himself but he had other duties and obligations that limited his actual involvement. He still managed to give what time he could. It was a politically astute move: the King and the Duke of York being seen in the streets, and not just seen but seen trying to extinguish the blaze.

James, Duke of York, was the younger brother of the King. Unlike his later collapse into the doldrums of ineptitude and inefficiency when he succeeded Charles as monarch, in 1666 he was a man of action, a renowned and successful soldier. And from the moment his appointment was confirmed he began to organise his forces.

Realising he could not be everywhere, James immediately appointed men he knew and trusted as his deputies. First, he created a command base for himself and his senior officers at Ely Place in Holborn.

Then, spinning out from the command base like spokes on a wheel, following the King's wishes, he established fire posts at various important positions around the city. These included Temple Bar, Shoe Lane and Clifford Inn's Gardens, along with several others, all at a sensible distance from the blazing town houses but with good links back to Ely Place.

Theoretically – although it is doubtful that the numbers of James's firefighters ever reached the quantity he desired – the fire posts were supposed to be run by the parish constables but overseen by a privy councillor or nobleman. Each of the controllers was aided by as many as three justices of the peace, a hundred civilian volunteers and thirty soldiers. Supplies of bread, beer and cheese were to be provided, up to the value of £5.

In total contrast to his later turpitude, at this time James was nothing if not a practical man and he set up a reward system, offering a one shilling gratuity to anyone who was particularly diligent in his services. Put together, it made up an effective system and further fire bases were soon established at vulnerable spots across the city.

James realised that he needed further help and ordered the counties of Kent, Surrey, Hertfordshire and Middlesex to send him as many members of their militias as they could spare. As well as fighting the fire, they would be used, he said, to prevent looting and rioting. By early afternoon the first of the militiamen had arrived in London.

* * *

Despite the efforts of the Duke of York, Monday was a seminal moment in the development of the fire. In the early light of dawn, it was clear that the fire, great as it had been and still was, had destroyed only a relatively small section of property inside the old Roman city walls. During the day, however, the easterly wind picked up and drove the flames relentlessly westwards.

By now the flames had gained control over most of the old city, houses and churches alike falling before its advance.

At Queenhithe, once a vital part of the port of London, a wide fire break was constructed across the marketplace. With Charles and James directing the work, it seemed as if salvation was at hand. However, by 10.00 a.m. the fire was just four houses distant from the old port.

The post office in Cloak Lane, off Dowgate, was destroyed early on Monday morning and the company halls of the cutlers, vintners and salters were also gutted during the day. The churches in the area north of Thames Street that were destroyed included the 'fair parish church' of St Michael Paternoster Royal, where Richard Whittington was buried.[3]

The Royal Exchange fell victim to the fire that day. Goods to an immense value had been stored there and the upper gallery of the building was filled with silks and golden cloths belonging to tradesmen and local officials. Stocks of pepper and spices belonging to the East India Company were destroyed in the basement of the building.

Both Charles and James spent several hours at Queenhithe that morning. The King thought that this was a good place to finally stop the fire and he personally employed a group of men, all eager to help and receive their share of the King's bounty for their efforts.

Several churches were destroyed that day, along with libraries and printing presses that had not long been set up. The company halls of the joiners and the plumbers met with the same fate. At least fourteen almshouses, institutions whose sole purpose was to provide warmth, care and shelter for the poor, met with similar disaster that September morning.

Charles left the scene at Queenhithe as soon as it became clear that the barrage was not going to work. He returned to the palace at Whitehall, where he appears to have spent many hours pondering on how to bring the affair to a successful conclusion.

James, as commander of the firefighting units, stayed on at the 'front line' of battle. Not afraid of getting his hands dirty, James quickly realised that the best way in which he could help was simply to be seen by the populace. John Evelyn was particularly struck by the behaviour of both Charles and James: 'It is not indeed imaginable how extraordinary the vigilance and activity of the King and Duke was, even labouring in person and being present, to command, order, reward and encourage workmen: by which he [meaning the King] gave affection to his people and gained theirs.'[4]

As if the threat of death and disaster were not enough, as the fire spread from street to street the city was subjected to what John Vincent described as 'noxious smells.' Londoners were used to the stink of the city but this was different.

The roads running alongside the Thames were an area where trades such as soap making and dyeing had become the principal trades. Steam, along with vile and stinking gasses from the process – discontinued or discarded as soon as the fire broke out – began to escape from the pits where boiling of materials to make the soap and other products happened.

James, like all of the other workmen, endured the stench. Kerchief across his nose and mouth, he ploughed on with what was clearly becoming a thankless task. Gaining the affection of the London people, however, was no mean achievement. Staunchly Parliamentarian, both during the Civil War and immediately afterwards, London was not exactly a nest of Royalists.

Charles and James knew that their positions were tenuous. Parliament and the people it represented had already killed one monarch. They did not want another regicide on their hands, so courting the diehard Republicans who still lingered in the city was a major preoccupation. Whether this was a motive for royal involvement in fighting the fire remains open for judgement.

* * *

Early on the Monday afternoon, the Duke of York called at the Navy Office in Seething Street – in other words the home of Samuel Pepys. He was looking for advice on how to manage such a huge conflagration and officers of the Navy, with their hard-learned skills dealing with fire on board one of the galleons, seemed a logical place to find it.

He found no-one at the office, no-one with the experience he needed anyway. Pepys was out in the city and anyone with sea-going experience was on the deck of his ship. James rode on, surrounded by his guards. He constantly talked with and encouraged the frightened people. Pepys returned home but the Duke was long gone.

James knew only too well that, despite most of them being underground, the wooden pipes that carried water through the streets had been burned to a crisp. He ordered that some of the city streets should be torn up in a desperate search for sewers. The water from the sewers might be filthy but it was a lot better than nothing.

But James was to be disappointed. The sewer water, which might have provided a degree of relief, barely existed. He gave a metaphorical shrug and moved on to Plan B, though as far as James and his officers were concerned, it would have seemed more like Plan X, Y or Z.

Foiled in his sewer water plan, James was forced to look elsewhere for an answer to the water problem. New lengths of elm were quickly cut, hollowed out and fashioned into replacement pipes. It was a desperate attempt and one that was doomed to failure. There was simply no water to be found, above or below ground.

In the seventeenth century nobody knew or realised that elm could be poisonous. In many respects their ignorance was not unlike the Roman predilection for lead piping in their aqueducts and water pipes or for lead in their face cream. The benefits, everyone felt, outweighed the drawbacks and so replacement elm piping it was.

Increasingly, it became obvious that there were only two options left to the firefighters. Both would be phenomenally expensive. Creating fire breaks was the first choice; abandoning the city to its fate was the second. Nobody, neither the firemen nor the royal planners, wanted the second option. The fire would be beaten.

Their efforts to put out the fire might be doomed but James and the King continued to make sure that they were seen in their efforts to quell the flames. The King was perhaps not as often on the scene as his brother but his efforts were still appreciated. *The London Gazette*, in the days after the fire, commented:

> It is easy to be imagined how many persons were necessitated to remove themselves and Goods into the open fields, where they were forced to continue some time which could not but work compassion in the beholders. The King and the Duke of York were frequent in consulting all ways for relieving those distressed persons.[5]

In command of a company of the King's Life Guards, soldiers actively fighting the fire, was the young Duke of Monmouth. Recently acknowledged as the natural son of King Charles II, Monmouth was handsome and popular with the people. Like James he was a man of action, popular with the public, ambitious and determined.

As the second night of the fire came to a close, directed and protected by Monmouth's troops, thousands of London citizens had already abandoned the city. Most of them were now living in the open air, in the fields surrounding the city. Some settled down in open land such as St Giles' Fields but the vast majority headed further out.

With their houses destroyed, the only canopy for these wailing refugees, wrote Thomas Vincent, was the sky that stretched out above their heads.[6]

Now, for the first time, people were subjected to a new problem – sore and burned feet. Such was the strength of the fire and the heat that fanned out before it that pavements and streets were turned into something resembling red-hot cinder beds. Painful as that was, it was not just the human body that was suffering, as Pepys soon discovered:

> Walked into Moorefields, our feet ready to burn, walking through the town among the hot coals, and find that full of people … And took up (which I keep beside me) a piece of glass of Mercer's Chapel in the street, where much more was, so melted and buckled with the heat of the fire, like parchment.[7]

It was a dangerous time, not simply because of the flames. The bare essentials of life were being threatened in a way that nobody had ever believed possible. Shelter, obviously, was at a premium and so, too, was respite from the terrifying heat that seemed to lie in wait and then burst out of almost every building which lined the streets.

Some relief might be obtained in the churches of the city but nearly eighty of these had already fallen to the flames. Thirty-five of them would never be rebuilt and replacing the rest would cost somewhere in the region of £360,000: '[It was] a colossal amount of money in an age when Pepys paid his cook £5 a year, and 5 shillings would buy a roast beef dinner for four in a tavern.'[8]

Finding drinking water was more difficult than finding water to put out the flames. Water was a basic requirement for life in the city but no-one had considered it or given it much thought before that night. It was there and you drank it when you were thirsty, a simple process that everyone had taken for granted over the years. Now there was no alternative but to look elsewhere for refreshment.

Butts of sugar lay discarded in the streets around the warehouses. Much of the contents of these bags and barrels was quickly snatched up and added to beer in order to sweeten it.

Even if ale houses and inns had been burned to the ground, beer was more freely available than water and soon became the accepted drink (sweetened, of course) for the gangs of women who were now working on trying to quell the fire. Many of them quickly became drunk on the mixture but they toiled on regardless.

Gradually but inexorably, the firefighters were becoming exhausted. The lucky ones may have been able to snatch an hour's sleep, or maybe just a few minutes' rest, but generally they battled on throughout the night. Men and women worked; some simply wandered, half asleep, almost unconscious on their feet.

Thomas Vincent was clear that, in his opinion, Monday night was one of the worst he and the people of London had ever endured: 'Monday night was a dreadful night when the wings of the night had shadowed the light of the heavenly bodies; there was no darkness of night in London, for the fire shines now round about with a fearful blaze, which yielded such light in the streets, as if it had been the sun at noon day."[9]

Early that evening, Samuel Pepys had returned to his house in Seething Lane, finding that both the office and his dwelling place were miraculously untouched by the fire. Pepys took no chances and decided he would not undress and go to bed. He would sleep on the floor, fully clothed.

The approach of the blazing inferno was still rapid. It was like the steady and insistent march of an advancing army in the background of Pepys's imagination. Imagination apart, it was a terrifying ordeal.

Pepys admitted in his diary that the thought of the fire destroying everything he knew and had worked for all his life was a horrendous experience.

Despite his fears, the diarist managed to catch an hour's troubled rest in his office, lying on the floor, covered by a blanket and with shoes on in case sudden flight was needed. And meanwhile, the wind roared and the fire spread.

Chapter 5

The Fire Leaps Forward

Regardless of the Reverend Thomas Vincent's beliefs and comments about the severity of Monday night's fire, Tuesday, day and night both, was later considered by everyone who was there to be the worst and most destructive period endured during the Great Fire of London.

The old city walls, which had stood for hundreds of years, gave up the ghost and finally acknowledged that they could offer no check on the raging fire. As the day progressed, flames burst through and over the ancient walls, moving on to destroy most of Cheapside, the Guildhall and, eventually and most dramatically of all, St Paul's Cathedral.

The cathedral was a huge landmark in the western part of the city but by September 1666 it was in dire need of repairs. As a consequence, the building was surrounded by scaffolding. John Evelyn believed that the long wooden structures, dozens upon dozens of them, a virtual forest of timber neatly tied against the sides and roofing of the building, greatly contributed to the disaster.

By some miracle, St Paul's escaped destruction during the day. However, its luck could not last forever and at dusk on the Tuesday evening, with fire raging all around the forecourt, fate eventually caught up with the complex that was St Paul's Cathedral.

The cathedral that existed in 1666 had originated in an old Saxon church, dating back to the period immediately following the Norman Conquest. The massive central tower, standing at 245 feet high, had been added in 1221. Crowned by a lead-covered timber spire, St Paul's was, at its tallest point, nearly 500 feet in height.

While never really used by Londoners, who preferred their own smaller churches and chapels, the cathedral was nonetheless an impressive sight and a landmark for visitors to the city. It also provided Londoners with a quick route or short cut to the northern parts of the city, a practice greatly condemned by Church authorities.

Over the years the original cathedral had been extended and added to, time and time again. Chapels and galleries of different heights and capacities, new and old adaptations, made it something of a warren for worshippers. However, the cathedral was still an impressive building and its destruction was a sight that no-one who witnessed it would ever forget.

Dusk saw no let-up in the strength of the wind, meaning that burning debris was caught and driven onwards, ahead of the flames. During the afternoon, large quantities of wood, paper, plaster and all of the other expected detritus of the fire had settled on the angled roofing of St Paul's. The defenders had no way of removing the rubbish from the various roofs and within half an hour of the sun setting the cathedral coverings were alight.

The wind was, of course, the real arsonist and destroyer of St Paul's, as it was with most of the houses and public buildings during the Great Fire. The wind roared, it swung, it died away and it smashed back at London with an intensity that amazed everyone. It was unpredictable and under its blanketing wildness the flames blazed away for hour after hour.

Finally, the roofing over the different parts of the cathedral collapsed, timbers and wooden blocks dropping like cannon balls through the air, falling hundreds of feet and destroying the floors beneath. The smoke, sparks and flames added to the chaos inside the building. To those watching, helpless and afraid, it seemed like the end of the world.

Below the mighty cathedral lay the old buildings of St Faith's church. It had served as a parish church for the stationers and booksellers who, for many years, had run and profited from their businesses in the courtyard of St Paul's. The area had been famous for its book selling since the days of Geoffrey Chaucer, the recent advent of the printing press making the area a logical home for writers and artists. Printing, binding and selling: it was all available in the environs of St Paul's.

Once the fire broke out back in Pudding Lane, and in the hours before it reached St Paul's, most of the stationers and booksellers had gathered up their stock and stored it in the church of St Faith. The books and printed sheafs filled the place from floor to ceiling, blocking exits and access to the upper floors and cutting off all forms of ventilation and clean air.

The booksellers did not realise that they were creating a fire risk. Now, when the various roofs collapsed, many stocks of paper were burned to a crisp. Some were destroyed in a matter of minutes, others smouldered for the next week or so.

Parts of the cathedral's masonry also began to disintegrate in the heat and the Duke of York's fire post in Coleman Street had to be abandoned. John Evelyn went to the cathedral soon after it exploded into flames and was appalled by what he discovered:

> The burning still rages; I went now on horseback and it was now gotten as far as the Inner Temple; all Fleet Street, old bailey, Ludgate Hill, Watling Street now flaming and most of it reduced to ashes. The stones of St Paul's flew like Granados, the Lead melting down the streets in a stream, and the very pavements of them glowing with fiery redness, so as no horse nor man was able to tread on them.[1]

Evelyn and other curious onlookers fell back before the waves of hot and steaming air. Nothing, it seemed, was safe from the intense heat, which probably caused more discomfort and damage than the flames.

Later analysis of melted pottery fragments that were found in an abandoned shop on Pudding Lane showed that the temperature of the fire in the area had reached as high as 1,700 degrees centigrade. Small wonder that Thomas Farriner and his household had such difficulty trying to escape the flames.[2]

That phenomenally high temperature was in Pudding Lane, the starting point for the fire. The blaze that destroyed St Paul's would probably have reached a considerably higher temperature.

* * *

It had now become obvious to the King and to his brother James that, with water not easily available inland, away from the Thames, the only way to contain the fire was to fall back on the old technique of creating fire breaks. Charles had always held this view and, unlike the Lord Mayor, Thomas Bludworth, he was not afraid to begin the process. He had the authority and the decisiveness to act. Whatever the consequences might be – paying for replacement buildings, putting up new roofs and so on – they were a problem that could be dealt with later.

The creation of large fire gaps had begun on the Tuesday, at Cripplegate, close to the Tower of London. Acting on the advice of sailors off the ships in London Dock, rather than pull down the houses, it was decided to use gunpowder to blast significantly bigger gaps than normal in the rows of houses. Speed was of the essence and it was a great deal quicker to blow up houses than it was to spend hours trying to pull them down using the traditional grappling hooks.

To begin with, the explosions frightened the Londoners, who thought that they were from the guns of invading French and Dutch sailors. They were quickly appraised of the truth and the explosions continued. More sailors soon arrived, press-ganged from the English fleet; then came soldiers who had been marshalled from their camps and depots. Samuel Pepys was clear about the value of what was going on: 'Now begins the process of blowing up houses in Tower Street, those next to the Tower, which at first did frighten people more than anything, but it stopped the fire where it was done.'[3]

Pepys may have been exaggerating the effect of gunpowder and explosives somewhat but blasting huge gaps in the terraces did manage to reduce the effect of flashover. It did not eliminate the problem altogether but by the end of the day incidents of the strange phenomena had been greatly reduced.

For want of a better description, it was a time of trial and error. Realising it was unenforceable, an edict passed only the day before, prohibiting carts coming into the city, was rescinded. Prices remained inordinately high but this was now a case where standing still would be fatal: you had to act to survive.

Tempers also ran high. As the day progressed, the idea that the fire was the work of a foreign power grew in magnitude. This was a belief which had begun life on Sunday, the first day of the fire, reinforced by the explosions around the Tower of London on Tuesday. It had started as a mere rumour but now people accepted the stories of invading troops as fact. Soon, it was a view that was almost universal in the city. And with that belief, of course, came a return to the violence of the previous day.

The newly appointed Portuguese ambassador was beaten and manhandled by a crowd of passersby who mistook him for a Dutchman. Rescued by the Lords Ashley and Hollis, who were standing at their fire post at Newgate Market and witnessed the assault, the non-English speaking ambassador retired gratefully to the sanctuary of Ashley's home. He knew he had come close to being lynched. Staying indoors was clearly the only way of avoiding the angry citizens – and that, naturally enough, carried its own risks.

One story in common circulation was that a woman who had been acting suspiciously had been seized and had her breasts cut off by an angry crowd of thugs. How much veracity there was in the story is unknown, but it spread like wildfire in the burning streets, terrifying both foreigners and native-born Britons.

Many of the foreign inhabitants of London sought refuge in the home of the Spanish ambassador at the Barbican. Catholic or Protestant, all were made welcome in an act of pure charity and humanity, in total contrast to the brutality of the streets.[4]

As the day wore on, twisting and bending the truth became something of a regular pastime. Yes, the fire had begun in a bakery on Pudding Lane, but now it became a bakery owned and run by a Dutchman. He had, so the word was, begun the fire deliberately. Of course, there was no evidence for this but for a short while it was believed implicitly.

Many people reported instances of foreigners being strung up from signposts, although no-one could produce any bodies. The old story of a combined Dutch and French army invading southern England was resurrected, only this time the army was marching on London. It was now 50,000 strong although, again, nobody had seen them come ashore.

The number of foreigners living in London at the time of the fire was in the thousands. Dutch, French, Spanish, Italian and many other different nationalities were represented.

The 'foreigners,' as they were known, were mainly skilled artisans, living and working as engravers, carpenters and, in particular, silk weavers. Their success had already caused complaints and disagreements from jealous English tradesmen; the fire simply gave them another avenue of attack.[5]

The foreign residents were easily identifiable by things like their choice of clothes and the national enclaves or city districts where they lived. Half believing the rumours and stories, government officials tried to stop foreigners – who might or might not be guerilla fighters and terrorists – from leaving the country. Orders were sent out to stop ships leaving ports along the south and east coasts of England.

James, Duke of York, was indefatigable in his efforts. He and the King had been in the city at daybreak on Tuesday and James remained in the saddle all day. He and the King worked particularly hard at helping to control the panic-stricken Londoners. Their safety and public opinion were, after all, their primary concern.

Often, a kind word or acknowledgement was enough to calm panic-stricken Londoners. However, Charles also carried a pouch brimming with golden guineas, from which he gave out coins as a reward to firefighters. His generosity was also an encouragement for many of the now homeless people of London, men and women who could see only a bleak future ahead of them.

As night fell, Charles finally went back to Whitehall. James remained working amongst the burning buildings. His efforts were remarkable, his popularity never greater.

At one stage James was trapped by the swirling flames and almost burned to death by the fire. He was forced to drop everything and flee before the flames. It was approaching midnight before he was finally persuaded to retire for the night.

As the day ended, the fires of destruction were still apparent. Nearly three-quarters of the city was in flames and even the King, his family and his courtiers, now fearing the worst, had begun to pack valuables onto boats and lighters, and ship them off to safer places like Twickenham.

The flight of the royals was not a great problem. As far as most Londoners were concerned, if the day had shown nothing else, it had highlighted the point that members of the royal family were as much potential victims of the fire as the lowest labourer or poorest servant girl. And they knew that the King would be back as soon as he had settled his family.

The major consolation left to the homeless citizens was simply that they were not alone in their misery. Their King had fought the fire along with the rest of them, often up to his knees in water and with the risk of death or injury from the fire hanging over his head. Now he and the other royals were suffering like them. That had to be a good omen: 'It is not indeed imaginable how extraordinary the vigilance and activity of the King and Duke was, even labouring in person, and being present, to command, order, reward and encourage workmen, by which he shewed his affection to his people, and gained theirs.'[6]

Affection was one thing, surviving the onslaught something totally different. Neither Charles nor James could be in all places at once. The people of the city had now reached the point where they needed to see success in the matter of quenching the fire, regardless of where it actually came from.

* * *

The firefighters believed that the River Fleet, which ran southwards across London before discharging into the Thames, would be their salvation. It would provide a natural barrier to the flames which, unable to go forward, would burn themselves out.

James, Duke of York, set up an additional cordon. This was a defensive barrier, between Holborn Bridge and the bridge over the Fleet. It was a line that would have to be held: fail to hold it and the whole of the city could be consumed by the flames. It was a thankless task, and a hopeless one at that, and it was only a matter of time before the fire leapt across the line between the bridges at Holborn and the Fleet.

People had been abandoning the city since Sunday, hundreds, if not thousands, of them wandering the streets until their turn arrived to pass through the gates in the old walls. There was no routine or structure to the evacuation; it was merely a case of who got to the gates first.

Outside the city walls, what waited for the newer refugees were empty fields, a few temporary shelters and crowds of people just like them. There were no facilities, either for cooking or for sanitary requirements.

Those who had carried prized possessions with them were obliged to just pile them up close to the spot where they had chosen to sleep and hope they would still be there in the morning. It was, of course, a thieves' paradise!

St Giles's Fields, Lincoln's Inn Fields, Hatton Gardens, Moorfields, even Tower Hill – it was the same sad story wherever anyone went. Fields of battered humanity, men and women too tired and shell-shocked to complain or cause problems, simply sat and stared at the burning city they had left behind them.

A sense of depression lay like a series of conjoined blankets across the refugee camps. Nobody knew what the future might hold and at this stage nobody could be bothered to think about it. The criminal element thought differently and, in the face of growing complaints, two companies of the city militia were detailed to patrol the makeshift camps. Their task was to maintain law and order and to prevent theft or looting.

Satisfied that he had done all he could, James retired to his temporary lodgings in the city. He at least had a roof over his head. The majority of the 'campers' in the London fields had, as Vincent had declared, no option but to sleep under the stars.

That Tuesday evening it was smoke which caused most concern amongst the fleeing citizens. The canopy of smoke was thick and it was poisonous, causing people to cough, choke and spit. Thomas Vincent recorded the problem in his usual florid manner:

> Now horrible is the flakes of fire that mount up in the sky, and the yellow smoke of London ascendeth [sic] up towards Heaven, like the smoke of a great furnace, a smoke so great as darkened the sun at midday. The cloud of smoke was so great that travellers did ride at noonday some miles together in the shadow thereof, though there were no other clouds besides to be seen in the sky.[7]

By 7.00 p.m. the fire had broken through the western wall and was heading down Fleet Street towards Chancery Lane. Samuel Pepys decided on another night of sleeping rough. He settled down on his office floor, wrapped a blanket around his body and, despite the pain in his feet, fell asleep.

Pepys had done all he could to protect his valuables, storing some of his goods in the cellar and sending some to friends in places like Bethnal Green and Woolwich.

Strangest of all, however, he had buried in the garden what he considered the most valuable resource: a full round, or wheel as it was known, of Parmesan cheese. Along with the cheese, Pepys buried a few barrels of wine. The garden at Seething Lane was a veritable treasure trove.

Doubtless Pepys loved his food but the rationale behind burying his cheese remains unknown. It was valuable, certainly. It was also heavy. Was the full wheel a prime target for thieves and looters? That was a distinct possibility. But was it really more valuable than his gold and silver? We will never know as he does not refer to the episode again in any of his diary entries.[8]

His house and office in Seething Lane survived the fire. Perhaps Pepys himself unearthed the 40-kilo wheel when things got back to normal. Or maybe some watching plunderer obtained for himself enough of the valuable and highly desirable commodity to keep himself fully supplied with breakfasts of cheese on toast for a year or so.

Early on the Wednesday morning, Samuel Pepys had more on his mind than cheese. New danger had come to Seething Lane – or so it seemed. He had retired relatively early:

> I lay down in the office again upon W Hewer's quilt, being mighty weary and sore in my feet with going till I was hardly able to stand. About 2.00 in the morning my wife calls me up and tells of new cries of 'Fyre,' it being come to Barkeing [sic] Church which is at the bottom of our lane. I up, and finding it so, resolved presently to take her away; and did, and took my gold, W Hewer and Jane down by Poundy's boat to Woolwich.[9]

No mention of cheese now, you will notice! The diarist had more important things on his mind. When Pepys and his boat came to Woolwich, they found no guard at the gates. No guard over a vital dockyard facility? That was contrary to all government and naval regulations.

An angry Pepys managed to get into the arsenal, however, charging his wife Elizabeth and William Hewer never to let the valuables out of their sight. Then he headed back upriver. Almost immediately, Pepys noticed a change.

The boatman was clearly having a difficult time keeping the wherry in midstream, the boat being constantly pushed towards the southern bank of the river. Normally it was something that would have been ignored. Not now.

Pepys had been expecting to find his house and the rest of the city in flames. He arrived back home at 7:00 a.m. to find that while the fire still burned in the rest of the city, his property remained intact. That was in complete contrast to so many Londoners, including Pepys's own father, who had lost his house and most of his possessions.

It became obvious that the wind had changed direction and, as the boatman had demonstrated with his inability to remain in mid-stream, was now blowing strongly to the south. This slice of luck, as Pepys quickly realised, might be the saving of the city.

The wind had played havoc for three days and although it had now changed direction and dropped a little in ferocity, it was currently driving the flames towards the river. If that continued, there was a fair chance of the fire blowing itself out.

Pepys and others might have been relieved but they were still not taking any chances. That evening, Wednesday 5 September, he brought in watchmen to keep an eye on the office and his house, providing them with bread and cheese – not the buried Parmesan. Pepys himself had his best night's rest for several days.

By midday on the Wednesday, the fire at Holborn Bridge was out and during the afternoon almost all of those in the west of the city had also been extinguished.

Only the blaze at Cripplegate continued to burn and this, along with a second outbreak at the Temple, was dealt with during the late afternoon or early evening.

Now that he was able to give attention to the condition and fate of the men and women out in the surrounding fields, Charles came up with a plan:

> His Majesty, fearing, less other orders might not yet have been sufficient, had commanded the Victualler of his Navy to send bread into Moorfields for the relief of the poor ... He sent in biscuits out of the Sea Store. It was found that the Markets had been already so well supplied that the people, being unaccustomed to that kind of bread, declined it, and so it was returned in great part to His Majesty's Stores, without any use made of it.[10]

The fire was not yet totally extinguished but the worst outbreaks had been contained. St Paul's was still smouldering, parts of it in flames, as were many of the larger, stone-built churches.

It was perhaps too early for mass celebrations but there was some light at the end of the tunnel and, in a fairly low-key manner, the people began to regale each other with stories of their miraculous escapes and the things they had seen and experienced.

There would be time to survey the damage in the days and weeks ahead. James probably never said it, but it remains easy to imagine his likely comments – for the moment, just be grateful that you are alive.

The Duke of York, like his brother, was keenly aware that sanctuary and survival from the flames were due to miraculous luck rather than any particular skill from the firefighters.

Chapter 6

Wednesday, Thursday, Good and Bad

On Wednesday 5 September Sir Thomas Bludworth reappeared. He had gone to ground following his ignominious remarks about the fire and the bodily functions of women, probably spending the time in his house. His failure to act earlier in the week had left problem solving and firefighting to the King and his brother James, Duke of York.

Now, with the danger almost gone, Bludworth could be seen directing the firefighting in the Cripplegate area of the city. It was more show than genuine effort and his antics fooled no-one.

Bludworth had been knighted in 1660 and was Alderman of Aldersgate from 1663 until 1682. His performance during the Great Fire, however, ruined his reputation forever. Although he continued his political career, he was often mocked and jeered at in public, and very few ever put faith in his actions and opinions ever again.

When Parliament met to discuss, amongst other things, Bludworth's behaviour during the fire, it was reported that his only contribution to ensuring the safety of 'his' city was to fill his chamber pot with liquid of a highly personal kind and throw it at the flames!

Samuel Pepys, never one to hold back an opinion, considered him 'a silly man, a very weak man.' King Charles's close friend Edward Ashley-Cooper went one step further, declaring him to be 'thrice vile.'[1]

Although Pepys and many others were quick to pick up on the change in Wednesday's wind and weather, the fire grumbled on throughout the day. No longer a roaring demagogue of a blaze, it was still strong enough to cause concerns. And, as everyone knew, there was always the possibility that it might rear up again.

A classic example of the fire reigniting or reappearing came during the Wednesday evening. Cinders, paper and other pieces of refuse from King's Bench Walk had managed to find a home for themselves on the roof of the Middle Temple Hall. Middle Temple was one of four Inns of Court where barristers were educated and trained. It had also been home to the Knights Templar, an organisation of soldier monks.

Despite people's hopes, beliefs and wishes, the fire was very much alive that Wednesday evening, dormant for the moment perhaps, but alive nonetheless. Now, suddenly, flames were kindled within Middle Temple Hall and burst into life. Within minutes the whole of the roof was ablaze.

James, Duke of York, was called to the scene, only to find the gates locked – to keep out looters, the lawyers of the Temple informed him. James, himself a bencher of the Inner Temple, was furious and was not going to allow himself to be treated like this.

It took some time to persuade the gate-keepers to let him in and then, when he saw that the only thing to do was to create a fire break by blowing up the Paper House, he was met by outright refusal from some of the lawyers and their servants. Tempers finally exploded and matters came to blows before, at last, James got his way. The Paper House was destroyed, the fire being extinguished in the early hours of Thursday morning.

At this point there was some relief for the members of the militia who had been fighting the blaze for the past two or three days. They were relieved by 200 militiamen from nearby areas who brought with them carts, wagons and tools for beating out the final flames. Fresh faces and fresh reserves of energy were sorely needed.

On Wednesday a royal proclamation was issued, ordering suppliers and farmers from outside London to bring in fresh supplies every day. Temporary markets were established at places like Tower Hill, Smithfield and Bishopsgate, even in far-off villages such as Islington and Ratcliff. Establishing aid and assistance for the homeless people of London was clearly more effectively done than fighting the flames of the Great Fire.

The city was still barely habitable. Pepys and John Evelyn wrote, several times, about the heat of the roads and pavements, complaining bitterly about the way they had burned their shoes and feet on the cobblestones.

The young schoolboy William Taswell added his opinion. Even on Thursday he found that the air was still 'Intensely warm' and that flammable goods which had been pushed into the Thames 'gave the impression that the river was on fire.'[2]

Writers like John Evelyn were more mature, more grounded in their opinions and views. One of Evelyn's greatest concerns was for the prisons and prisoners of the city: 'The vast yron [iron] chaines of the City streets, vast hinges, bars and gates of Prisons were many of them melted and reduc'd to cinders by the vehement heats.'[3]

Evelyn was right to be concerned. Over the four days of the fire several London prisons, places such as the famous Bridewell, were damaged or totally destroyed. Many of the inmates, naturally enough, seized the opportunity to escape and disappear into the depths of burning London.

Fleet Prison, on the bank of the Thames, was used mainly as a debtor's jail, the original edifice dating back to the twelfth century. Now it was burned to the ground. Chaos reigned and many of the inmates took the opportunity to 'disappear' from the prison confines. Most of them, being debtors rather than hardened criminals, were either recaptured or gave themselves up after a week or so on the run.

Newgate was badly damaged but it survived the fire, being rebuilt and modified over the next few months. When the fire first approached Newgate Prison, the jailors marched their prisoners out of the burning building, intending to take them to a safe haven at Southwark. It was a hopeless task. Many of the prisoners never made it, slipping quietly away when the jailors' backs were turned.

The crime rate in London does not seem to have been increased greatly by the escaping prisoners but the looting and pilfering of property and belongings then going on does tend to distort the figures. The decision to introduce the temporary armistice for looters who had been caught was also a contributing factor to what seemed – considering the circumstances – a relatively low crime rate.

* * *

By Wednesday nightfall the fire might have passed beyond the point of maximum danger but the city and its inhabitants were not yet out of the woods. Thomas Vincent, after an almost statutory acknowledgement of God's good grace in easing the strength and direction of the wind, was quick to acknowledge the latest fear amongst the people:

> But on the Wednesday night, when the people late of London, now of the fields, hoped to get a little rest on the ground, where they had spread their beds, a more dreadful fear falls upon them then they had before, through a rumour that the French were coming armed against them to cut their throats and spoil them of what they had saved out of the fire.[4]

There had been several invasion scares before, notably on the Sunday and Monday, but this particular rumour seemed to strike a chord with the refugees. The difference now was that the people of London had endured three nights of terror and disaster. They had seen their houses and businesses burned and destroyed. Their security had been questioned and found wanting. They were in no fit state to accept any more dangers: 'They were now naked and weak, and in ill condition to defend themselves, and the hearts, especially of the females, do quake and tremble and are ready to die within them.'[5]

Despite their fear, a great many displaced citizens were consumed by fury. They had suffered enough and were damned if they were going to let the French pillage their few remaining possessions.

A call to arms was effectively answered, people grabbing broomsticks, axes, rakes and whatever other makeshift weapons they could lay hands on. The French invasion force never materialised and when the rumour was finally dispelled as false, the relief amongst the men and women camping out in the fields was tangible.

Thursday began with a degree of hope that had been missing in the city for some days. It was an emotion that was soon squashed. St Paul's was still on fire, flames licking at the clouds and sky. Other buildings, notably stone or brick-built, continued to defy the flames but the heat thrown out from these monoliths was not reassuring. The books and manuscripts stored by the booksellers in St Faith's chapel also continued to smoulder and burn quietly.

It remains unclear how the fire managed to invade the chapel of St Faith's, some accounts declaring that it forced its way in through the chapel windows, others believing that the books caught fire when timbers and masonry from St Paul's fell through the flooring and the arches of the cathedral. Bedding and other flammable materials that had been stored and piled up against the outer wall of the cathedral might also have been a cause. There were more than enough options to choose from.

* * *

Before the day was out dozens of sightseers, including Samuel Pepys and John Evelyn, had visited the remains of St Paul's Cathedral. The burned-out shell of the building provided an awful spectacle, much of it still home to final burning remnants of fire.

However, the young and still innocent William Taswell recorded a far more dreadful vision than the two famous diarists. Like Pepys and Evelyn, he had been to the cathedral, filling his pockets with pieces of bell metal and pausing to stare at the new-fangled fire engines which had been called from all parts of the city and were now playing water onto the last of the burning buildings. Then he encountered a sight which was to remain with him for many years:

> Near the east wall of St Paul's a human body presented itself to me, parched up as it were, with the flames; whole as to skin, meagre as to flesh, yellow in colour. This was an old decrepit woman who fled here for safety, imagining the flames would not have reached her there. Her clothes were burnt, and every limb reduced to a coal.[6]

Descriptions of dead bodies and records of death during the Great Fire of London are minimal. According to witness recollections only six people died in the fire, Taswell's sighting of a body being one, the servant girl of Thomas Farriner another.

The only 'named' victim of the fire was Paul Lowell, an eighty-year-old watchmaker who refused to leave his Westminster house. His bones and his keys were all that was left of him when the fire was extinguished.

Considering the severity of the blaze and the rapidity with which it spread, if the figure of just six victims is correct then it is an amazingly low death toll. However, intense heat does strange things to human flesh. Bodies shrink and sometimes become a mass of carbon. What is left usually looks more like burned wood or limestone – easily mistaken in the wake of a huge conflagration like the Fire of London. Often the remains disintegrate when touched, leaving only ash behind.

It is possible that the difficulty of identifying remains as human bodies has restricted the official number of the dead to just six. From this distance in time it is difficult to make a judgement but six deaths in the five days of the fire seems to be an inordinately low number.

Establishing an exact total of deaths has been made more difficult by the non-appearance of the Rolls or Bills of Mortality, London's daily record of deaths in the city. These documents were normally printed and published on a printing press held in the Parish Clerks Hall on Broad Lane. With the fire fast approaching the clerks in charge of the Rolls fled, taking with them whatever ledgers and documents they could.

However, the great books containing the initial records before publication were too heavy and were left to burn. Consequently, nothing relating to Rolls or Bills of Mortality was published for the three weeks immediately following the end of the fire.[7]

Even if the statutory rolls had been published, it remains doubtful that every death would have been recorded. The deaths of working class and middle class citizens were not always recorded and as the fire wiped out working-class areas of the city, destroying the workers' living quarters and, probably, the labourers themselves, many such instances might have slipped through the net.

Such was the heat of the fire that human remains were likely to have been destroyed, atomised as we would now say. With many residents not registered, their presence in the city left unrecorded, the only proof of their demise would have come from friends or colleagues. So, just six fatalities? Taking all of the issues into consideration, a more accurate death toll would probably have been in the high hundreds.[8]

There were many deaths in the period following the extinguishing of the fire. Homeless citizens were forced to spend months in temporary accommodation such as tented villages or even the burned-out shells of their houses. They were natural targets for disease and quickly became victims of the cold and weather.

To add more discomfort to the plight of the homeless, heavy rain set in soon after the fire was put out. The Puritans and other radical religious groups were only too happy to attribute the coming of the rain to God's judgement but, regardless of belief, for most people the downpour was simply a case of too little, too late.

If the human death toll was unexpectedly low, the killing of animals, birds, pets and the like was inordinately high. Pepys, as we have seen, wrote memorably about the death of a flock of unsuspecting pigeons but his most poignant piece has to be about the fate of a cat: 'I also did see a poor Catt taken out of a hole in the chimney joyning [sic] to the wall of the Exchange, with the hair all burned off the body and yet alive.'[9]

The destruction of property and the end of the style of life that had been previously enjoyed by residents and visitors alike were certainly important changes to emerge from the remains of the disaster. At first glance it appeared as if the city was irrevocably damaged. Certainly the old London had gone, its passing lamented by some, celebrated by others:

> Thus fell [sic] great London, that ancient city, that populous city! London, which was the Queen city of the land, and as famous as most cities in the world ... The merchants had left the Royal Exchange; the buyers and sellers have now forsaken the streets. The glory of London is now fled away like a bird, the trade of London is shattered and broken to pieces; her delights also are vanished and pleasant things laid waste.[10]

What Thomas Vincent had in mind when he mentioned 'pleasant things' in the above passage were innocent things like easy, elegant dancing and listening to 'sweet music' played on lyres. Changes would come to both sides of the cultural divide.

There would be, Vincent declared, no more amorous affairs between non-married couples – highly significant for a religious fanatic like him. At the other extreme, there were now precious few houses of worship in which to sing the glory of God.

Others, with more basic needs, would undoubtedly have lamented the destruction of houses of ill repute, an excess of wine and ladies of the night. Those brothels and taverns that had survived would reap a grim but welcome harvest in the months ahead.

The Reverend Thomas Vincent was typical of the sharp Puritan edge to life in late Stuart London. His picture of a defeated and abandoned city is a touching one, regardless of your stance and position: 'And in the places where God hath been served, and his servants hath lived, now nettles are growing; owls are screeching; thieves and cut throats are lurking; a sad face there is now in the ruinous part of London.'[11]

In the weeks and months ahead, there would be time to allocate blame and for the designing of plans for rebuilding the city. But that was in the future. For the moment the fire was out. It was time to breathe a sigh of relief and ponder on what might have happened.

The death toll incurred during the fire might have been amazingly low but nearly a hundred workers died in the 'rebuilding' of the city. These were mainly accidents: men falling from scaffolding or crushed by loose bricks and rogue masonry. They, too, should be included in the death toll of the fire. Again, the figure remains a little vague but, all in all, the real death toll of the Great Fire of London has to be in the thousands.[12]

* * *

In just four days the Great Fire of London had destroyed 373 acres of land, buildings and property within the walls of the old city, and a further 63 acres outside. Some 13,200 houses, mainly made of wattle and daub, had been burned or pulled down to create fire breaks, making well over 80,000 people homeless and destitute.

Fleeing London was no easy task. Eight narrow gates in the original Roman wall were the only way out of the burning city and the crush of people clustered around these exits was dramatic in the extreme. Men fought, women were pushed to the ground and children were trampled in the rush to get through the gates. Behind them the city burned.

Along with the homes of the fleeing workers, by the time the fire was extinguished civic buildings such as the Guildhall and the Royal Exchange had been destroyed, along with eighty-seven parish churches and six chapels. The flames did not reach the royal palace at Whitehall but at one stage it seemed highly likely that the King's chief residence would go up in flames like the rest of the city.

Serious damage to four stone bridges across the rivers Thames and Fleet continued to make communication between various parts of the city more than a little difficult for some after the fire was put out.

London Bridge, which at one stage had been in danger of complete destruction, escaped with one third of its structure lost and considerable damage sustained by the rows of shops and houses that lined the roadway across the Thames.

Saving recognised structures such as London Bridge and the Palace at Whitehall was down to luck rather than judgement. It was a common enough story. Whichever way you looked at it, however, the fire was a disaster of immense magnitude.

By the weekend of 9–10 September people were attempting to get back to normal. It was not easy in a city half destroyed by fire and with a populace crippled by emotional trauma. In many parts of the city, fire still smouldered in the remains of the battered, burned-out buildings. Samuel Pepys, however, did his best to resume a normal pattern of life: 'I to church, where our parson made a melancholy but good sermon – and many, and most, in the church cried, especially the women.'[13]

A week later, on 17 September, he was writing in his diary about his own personal condition and behaviour in the face of the disaster. He had survived. So had his wife, Elizabeth, and his house, along with its staff. There was a clear element of smugness about Samuel Pepys and in his diary entries at that moment in time: 'Up betimes, and shaved myself after a week's growth; but Lord, how ugly I was yesterday and how fine today.'[14]

The fire might have been extinguished, the danger relegated to history, but the city of London had a long way to go before anything even remotely resembling normality returned. Some of the rebuilding took fifty years to complete; a number of the great churches were never rebuilt at all.

All in all, redesigning and rebuilding London became a trail of immense strain and sorrow. And the journey began with a desperate search for scapegoats. They were relatively easy to find in a city still reeling from shock and distress.

Chapter 7

Victims, Villains and Heroes

Victims? Arguably the whole population of London, circa 1666, can be herded into this category. People lost their homes, some lost their lives, many lost their occupations and their livelihoods. Most of the citizens from 1666, as individuals, have slipped beyond our memories. It is, perhaps, time to bring some of them back.

The city of London in the Restoration period seems, with the benefit of hindsight, to have been set in a state of perpetual unrest. Trouble abounded around every street corner. If it wasn't being caused by the young rakes of the new permissive society or by women with recently discovered rights and desires, then riot and public argument were down to the Puritans and other hard-core religious sects left over from the time of Oliver Cromwell and the Commonwealth.

Or perhaps much of the disharmony came from former Parliamentary officers like Colonel John Rathbone who rebelled against the King on his Restoration in 1660. Rathbone was determined to re-establish the Commonwealth and was more than content to use violence to achieve his aim. There were many like him, but memories of the Civil War were too close and the idea of another insurrection was, for the moment, shelved.

Whatever the cause, London was throbbing with energy and discontent. The city was full of eager individuals, all with new ideas and plans. Few would have recognised it as such but the Great Fire, when it came, was the physical manifestation of a brave new world beginning to stretch and grow.

For the ten years between the Restoration of the Monarchy and the Great Fire of London, the city was full of vibrant life. Art and literature flourished, the novel beginning to take its place at the forefront of people's interest. Science and a desire to explore the natural world became significant factors. The Royal Society was founded in 1662, the Royal Observatory at Greenwich just a few years later.

In cities like London, inns and taverns provided warmth and bonhomie. For the first time people were deliberately going out to enjoy themselves for the evening rather than using inns as places to stay over as part of a journey. Then there were the famous coffee houses.

The first known coffee house in Britain was opened in 1652, just before the Restoration. By the time Charles returned to the throne their popularity had become immense. Known as Penny Universities – coffee was a penny and the shops were always full of intellectuals debating, discussing and lecturing on their work – the coffee house culture was another element to the vibrancy of cities like London. It was, in many respects, a reaction against the Puritan values of the Commonwealth, a reaction that people embraced with charm and ease.

As might be expected, Samuel Pepys caught perfectly the mood of the city during the fire and the months immediately afterwards. He had the words and the education to express himself but hundreds of others, without his skills – despite their inabilities, still victims all – undoubtedly felt the same:

> Walked into Moorfields, our feet ready to burn, walking through the town among hot coles [sic]. Drank there, and paid twopence for a plain penny loaf. Thence homeward, having passed through Cheapside and Newgate Market, all burned – and seen Antony Joyce's house in fire ... And I had forgot almost the day of the week.[1]

Over-priced food and drink were a common experience at this time, as were extortionate prices to hire carts, coaches and rowing boats. Londoners paid the increased prices on transport and provisions because they had no alternative. They wanted to escape, they wanted to live, and they would pay almost anything to achieve those ends.

Realistically, that desire to get away was one reason for the low death toll. People were more concerned with saving their own skins than they were with fighting the fire. It also made them classic victims at the hands of unscrupulous merchants, bakers, shop-owners and the like.

The playwright James Shirley and his wife both died in October 1666, not burned to death but from exposure and emotional pressure as a result of having to leave their home. They had been living for a month in a canvas tent, totally unsuitable accommodation for such elderly individuals.

Shirley had been a successful dramatist, a favourite of Queen Henrietta Maria and King Charles I until, in 1642, the Parliamentary rulers of London closed all of the London theatres. Shirley never recovered and losing his house in the Great Fire was pretty much the last straw for this emotionally fragile man.

Religious warnings and prophesies had abounded in London ten or twenty years before the fire. They were vivid, they were real, and they predated any fear of invasion by the Catholics, the French or the Dutch. The city was doomed, the prophets claimed, destined for destruction and it would soon be destroyed by fire.

Some prophesies even predicted, with surprising accuracy, the date of the great conflagration that was coming. It would strike in September 1666, proclaimed one Richard Edlin. It was, he said, God's vengeance for the sinful and heretical nature of the city's inhabitants. The accuracy of the date, a matter of pure chance, gave added weight to Edlin's reputation as a prophet and to the belief that this was no ordinary fire. When, perfectly on time, the fire arrived, the prophets of doom declared that its arrival and its effects had all been planned by a vengeful God.

The main image, used so freely and so effectively by the forecasters of doom, was the Biblical story of Sodom and Gomorrah. Just as the twin cities had been destroyed by fire and pestilence, proclaimed the predictors of doom, so sinful London would be destroyed as well.

Catholics, unpopular and feared since the days of Bloody Mary, Queen Mary I, were quickly identified and then vilified as the group most capable of making religious prophesies about the fate of London. From them came the prophesies and then, arguably, the task of setting them in motion. As Thomas Vincent declared:

> This doth smell of a Popish design, hatched in the same place where the Gunpowder Plot was contrived, only that this was more successful. The world sufficiently knows how correspondent this is to popish principles and practices; those who would intentionally blow up King and Parliament by gun-powder might (without any scruples of their kind of conscience) actually burn an [sic] heretical city (as they count it) into ashes.[2]

As a consequence, many believed that the fire was the work of Catholic agitators, possibly aided by the Dutch or French, both powers intent on exacting revenge for recent military defeats or setbacks. Between them all, the idea of overthrowing the country's Protestant government was not something that could be easily dismissed.

For fifty or so years, shades of the Catholic-instigated Gunpowder Plot of 1605, mixed with a large dose of wild Biblical doom, had hung in the air above England like a potent and dangerous nightmare. Now there was the distinct possibility that it had become reality.

Some of the more radical Protestant groups went a stage further. They genuinely believed that the fire was the work of James, Duke of York. He was a known supporter and friend of the Catholic Church, and his energy in driving forward his beliefs was renowned. He had set the fire, the radicals declared, deliberately trying to destroy the capital of his brother, the King, and cloaking his actions in a veneer of concern and assistance.

Everyone knew that while the fire raged, James kept appearing at almost every danger point, often putting himself at serious risk. That was his role, the role he had willingly taken on. But to many, it was not courage or a desire to save the city: it was simply his willingness to gain every last second of enjoyment from seeing London burn. The Duke of York, hero and villain – it makes an interesting, if unrealistic, proposal.

It was utter nonsense, of course, but there were many people who genuinely believed James and the Catholics were to blame. They were totally convinced and unswerving, sure that they were right in their judgement. Not even the gallant performance of the Duke as he fought the blaze could change their opinions.

It remains something of a judgement call but the bigoted and one-eyed approach of such individuals indicates that they, or people like them, were the perpetrators of the various assaults on foreigners during the fire.

Foreigners were, of course, natural victims. It was not always easy to spot a Catholic but identifying a Swede, a Frenchman or a Dutchman, from the way they dressed, spoke and acted, was relatively simple.

Italians, Spanish, Germans, Flemings: the range of foreigners living and working in London was vast, despite the fact that the English, Londoners in particular, were noted for their lack of hospitality. From young children to aged and infirm old men, the response to almost any approach by a Dutchman – Hollanders as they were known – was invariably a mouthful of abuse and the suggestion that they pack up and go home.

When such xenophobic, racist opinions were backed up by inexplicable happenings like the escape from destruction of the Dutch church at Austin Friars – why should it survive intact when eighty-seven other churches were burned and destroyed? – it was easy to conjure a reason. The fire had been set by the Dutch!

* * *

A small number of valuable paintings were destroyed before the fire was finally put out. The works of art might well be regarded as a somewhat strange group of inanimate objects to include in a list of victims but, nonetheless, they were still helpless and hapless objects in the face of grave danger.

With the fire destroying what were, in the main, working-class communities, the destruction of art works, of local or national importance, was never going to be enormous. Collections of paintings did not feature significantly on the list of priorities for the workers of London – tomorrow's dinner or tonight's beer were of much more importance. Church wall paintings, frescos and statuettes were a different matter and seem, in the main, to have been the principal victims. There were, as might be expected, the occasional exception or two.

Shortly before 2 September, a painting by Hans Holbein, court painter to Henry VIII, had just been bought from a goldsmith living and working on London Bridge. A sum of £100 was agreed for the painting but, within days, the fire broke out and the painting was destroyed.

Two more Holbein masterpieces – *The Triumph of Riches* and *The Triumph of Poverty* – were burned in the Steelyard area of the city, although it was whispered that the paintings had been secretly saved. They had, said the rumour, been taken to Europe and were never returned to London or any part of the British Isles.

Samuel Pepys did remark on the fate of some of the statues and wall coverings in places like Thomas Gresham's magnificent Royal Exchange but his comment was, really, little more than an aside. London art seems to have got off relatively lightly in the Great Fire: 'The Exchange a sad sight, nothing standing there of all the statues and pillars but Sir Thomas Gresham's picture in the corner.'[3]

St Paul's Cathedral, seemingly immune to the fire for so long, eventually erupted in a seething mass of flames on the Tuesday evening. And when it burned it took with it some of the finest monuments in London's history. These included the tombs of King Ethelred the Unready, and the saints Erkenwald and Sebba, along with many monuments to the long-dead nobles of the city.

Valuable records, minutes and civic collections were lost to the fire, leaving the city with unfilled or unfinished parts of its history. These included the Rolls or Bills of Mortality that later became so important in assessing the number of deaths in 1666.

Pepys was right to comment on the destruction of the Royal Exchange and its contents. The Exchange was wiped out by the fire on Monday 3 September as the flames began to make inroads into the heart of the city.

But the Exchange was not just another glorious building that met its end. The shops occupying its upper floors housed thousands of pounds worth of goods such as linen and silk. Far beyond the financial range of the ordinary inhabitant of the city, the silks were exquisite items that would have been at home in any wealthy woman's apartment.

Fear remained rampant, right to the end of the fire. Lady Anne Herbert wrote to her cousin that she was almost out of her wits with terror: 'We did look to be killed every hour.' Sometimes the fear was more specific.

Henry Griffith turned his emotions to anger, raging in a letter about villains who had stolen his father's trunk. It had been carried out to the fields for safety but when Griffith arrived to reclaim his possessions there was no sign of the trunk or its contents. Dozens of similar stories quickly displaced the romantic notion that Londoners were all in it together.[4]

Apart from magnificent examples of architecture found in places like the Royal Exchange and St Paul's Cathedral, dozens of other historic buildings were also burned in the raging inferno. These included a number of old and well-established taverns or inns. Places such as The Three Cranes Tavern, the city's oldest riverside inn, soundly disliked by Samuel Pepys but loved by many others, were among the first to go.

Another famous tavern to burn was The Boar's Head, a drinking house where Elizabethan playwrights like Shakespeare, Ben Jonson and Kit Marlowe used to spend much of their free time.

Shakespeare captured the atmosphere of the tavern for posterity in his plays about Henry IV and Henry V. The Boar's Head, as he portrayed it, was a simple enough place but he commemorated it as one of the favourite drinking dens of Sir John Falstaff.

The Boar's Head was the tavern where Doll Tearsheet and Mistress Quickly kept everyone in order and it remains obvious from reading the plays, along with seeing them performed on stage, that the author had spent a considerable amount of time within its walls. Not any longer.

Other notable locations to suffer the ultimate fate included the house of Richard 'Dick' Whittington, three times Lord Mayor of the city, and the Steelyard, a city within the city, where Sir Francis Drake once had a house and which was now home to the warehouses of the fabulous wealthy Hansa merchants. The Great Fire did not discriminate where people and places were concerned.

Baynard's Castle, a large, stone-built house which marked the western limit of the city, had been built by one of William the Conqueror's noblemen. It had stood there for centuries, the military counterpart to the Tower of London on the eastern edge of the city, and was generally thought to be indestructible. But this was wrong.

Baynard's Castle caught fire on the Monday evening and continued to burn all night. Samuel Wiseman wrote about its demise: 'The flinty walls of Baynard's strong built castle, thought by the inhabitants that westward dwelt, a powerful garrison against the flames, yielded like a paper building to the fire.'[5]

And then, inevitably, came the villains of the piece. The people of London were still trying desperately to escape the flames but they, and the authorities, still found time to point the finger of blame at anyone who had shown themselves to be vulnerable.

* * *

Perhaps the best-known example of a 'fire villain' was Robert Hubert, a Frenchman from Rouen who was then living and working as a silversmith in London.

What makes Hubert's case so interesting is the fact that within a few weeks of the fire's outbreak he was in custody, claiming to be the leader of over twenty similar conspirators. He had not been arrested or apprehended but had turned himself in, confessing to the authorities that he had begun the conflagration.

Robert Hubert was the perfect scapegoat, the ultimate victim, and that was something which the authorities needed desperately as Londoners began making accusations in all directions.

Quickly brought to trial, the case of Robert Hubert fascinated everyone. Whether he qualifies as a victim or a villain is a matter of personal choice.

Under cross-examination, Hubert came across as a man who was clearly disturbed or mentally unbalanced. He changed his story several times but began with an outright lie. He had just returned from Sweden, he claimed, his ship having just tied up at St Katherine's Tower. His story then took a bizarre turn.

Early on the morning of Sunday 2 September Hubert and a friend, one Stephen Peidloe, apparently found themselves outside Farriner's bakery. Peidloe handed Hubert a fire ball, which he promptly threw into the house, through an open window. He then claimed to have manoeuvred it into the most effective position with the help of a long pole.

It was all pure fantasy. As Thomas Farriner swore when called to give evidence, there was no such window in the bakery. Desperate as he was to deny any responsibility for the debacle, Farriner's evidence was the truth. It could and should have helped declare Hubert innocent.

Evidence clearly showing Hubert to be innocent continued to pile up. There was no fire bomb, no gang of eager conspirators. No ship had arrived from Sweden during the past month and Peidloe did not exist. He was simply a figment of the Frenchman's imagination. As the story unfolded and cross-examination became more intense, Hubert changed his story again and again. In fact, he changed it so many times, adding bits and sometimes altering the whole fabric of his tale, that the finished article bore no similarity whatsoever to the original.

Clearly the man was not just a fabricator of untruths. Lying was in his nature and he was a pathological inventor of fanciful tales that gave him fame and notoriety, even if they meant he might have to face the ultimate punishment. Careful examination revealed that one fact was true. He had not been in London either prior to or during the fire. But he had not been in Sweden – he had been in France. And that, given the growing hatred for both the French and Dutch, was possibly not the correct route to take. Time for another change of direction.

It soon became common public knowledge that Hubert had been visiting his father when the fire broke out. He did not return to England until the blazing inferno was almost extinguished. There was no way he could have been involved in any aspect of setting or encouraging the fire.

Colleagues at the watchmaker and silversmith's shop where he earned his living testified that he was a fantasist with something of a death wish. Finally realising the precarious nature of his position, Hubert admitted that everything he had said had been a pack of lies. Unfortunately for him it was now too late.

The press and the public were demanding justice and some form of reaction against the Catholics. The fact that Hubert was actually a Huguenot was irrelevant. The court found him guilty and Robert Hubert was duly hanged at Tyburn some six weeks after the fire had begun. It was, everybody knew, a clear case of revenge for the supposed assault on the city but it was certainly not justice.

* * *

As the Great Fire finally died away, one man – and one man only – was qualified to take up the role of 'the most unpopular man in London'. That man, of course, was Sir Thomas Bludworth, Lord Mayor of the city.

Street life in London did not really change much, even after the fire – as this early Victorian photo shows.

ord Mayor of London, the inept
homas Bludworth.

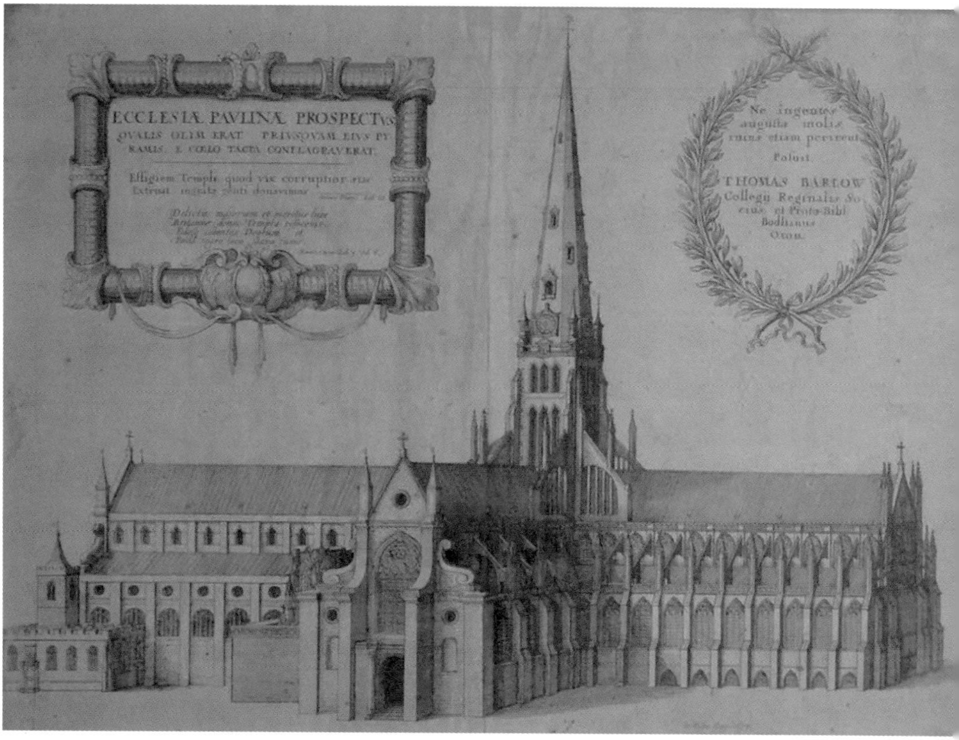

Old St Paul's.

Samuel Pepys, diarist and recorder of the fire.

Elizabeth Pepys, wife of Samuel Pepys.

enteenth-century fire engine.

London in flames.

The flames grow and London burns.

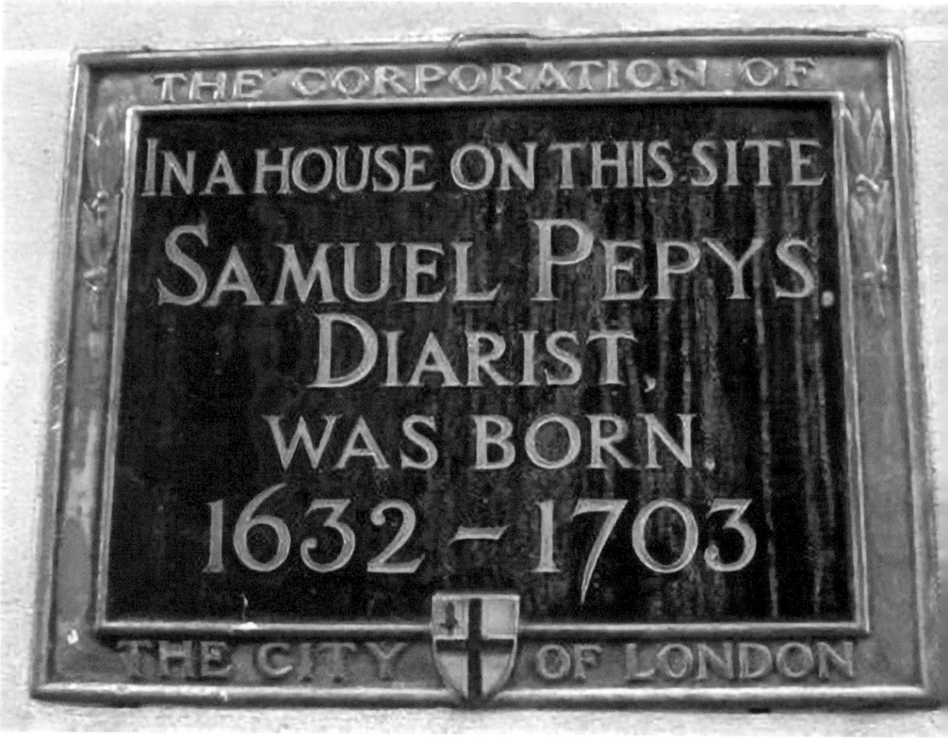

THE CORPORATION OF
IN A HOUSE ON THIS SITE
SAMUEL PEPYS,
DIARIST,
WAS BORN
1632 – 1703
THE CITY OF LONDON

Plaque marking the birthplace of Pepys.

King Charles II, by John Michael Wright.

early portrait shows James, Duke of York, with his father Charles I.

Contemporary drawing of Robert Hubert, supposed arsonist.

The Great Fire of London by unknown artist.

ames, Duke of York.

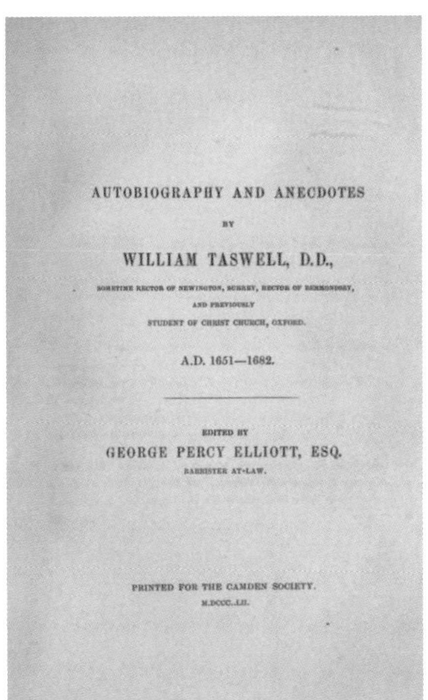

AUTOBIOGRAPHY AND ANECDOTES

BY

WILLIAM TASWELL, D.D.,

SOMETIME RECTOR OF NEWINGTON, SURREY, RECTOR OF BERMONDSEY,

AND PREVIOUSLY

STUDENT OF CHRIST CHURCH, OXFORD.

A.D. 1651—1682.

EDITED BY

GEORGE PERCY ELLIOTT, ESQ.

BARRISTER AT-LAW.

PRINTED FOR THE CAMDEN SOCIETY.

M.DCCC.LII.

Title page of Taswell's book about the disaster.

scaping the fire by boat.

Fire.

Architect Christopher Wren by Godfrey Kneller 1711.

irehooks used to create fire breaks.

Tower of London.

Fishmongers' Hall, the first large building to catch fire.

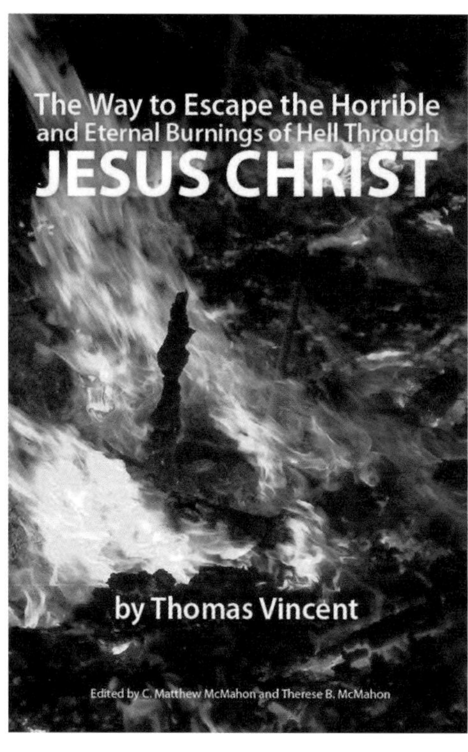

Cover of one of Thomas Vincent's books.

The fire burns on.

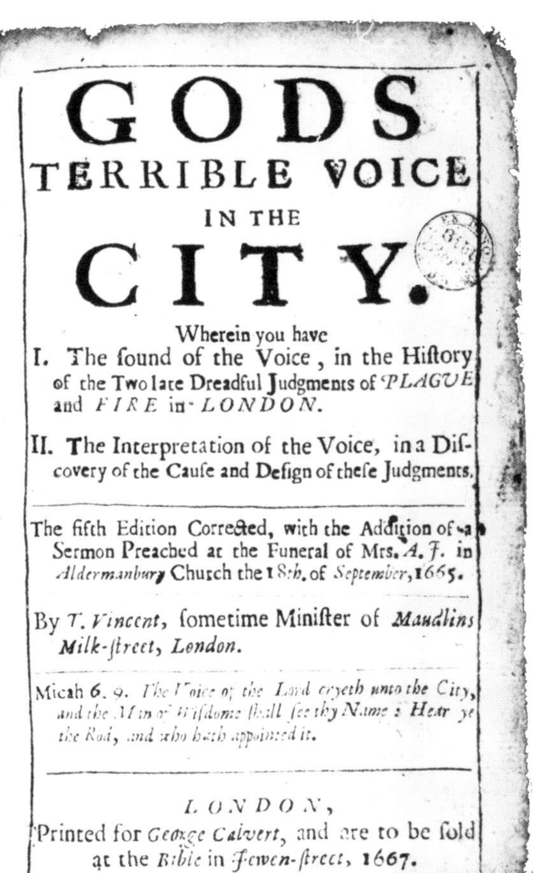

GODS TERRIBLE VOICE IN THE CITY.

Wherein you have

I. The ſound of the Voice, in the Hiſtory of the Two late Dreadful Judgments of *PLAGUE* and *FIRE* in *LONDON*.

II. The Interpretation of the Voice, in a Diſcovery of the Cauſe and Deſign of theſe Judgments.

The fifth Edition Corrected, with the Addition of a Sermon Preached at the Funeral of Mrs. *A. J.* in *Aldermanbury* Church the 18th. of *September*, 1665.

By *T. Vincent*, ſometime Miniſter of *Maudlins Milk-ſtreet, London.*

Micah 6. 9. *The Voice of the Lord cryeth unto the City, and the Man of Wiſdome ſhall ſee thy Name: Hear ye the Rod, and who hath appointed it.*

LONDON,

Printed for *George Calvert*, and are to be ſold at the *Bible* in *Jewen-ſtreet*, 1667.

Newspaper report of the fire.

Old print of Fleet Prison, one of several jails to burn in the fire.

Old outside oven like the one in Farriner's bakery.

Inside the Monument , a print from *The Graphic* of 1891.

The Monument.

Seething Lane, where the fire began.

Surviving section of the Old Roman walls of London.

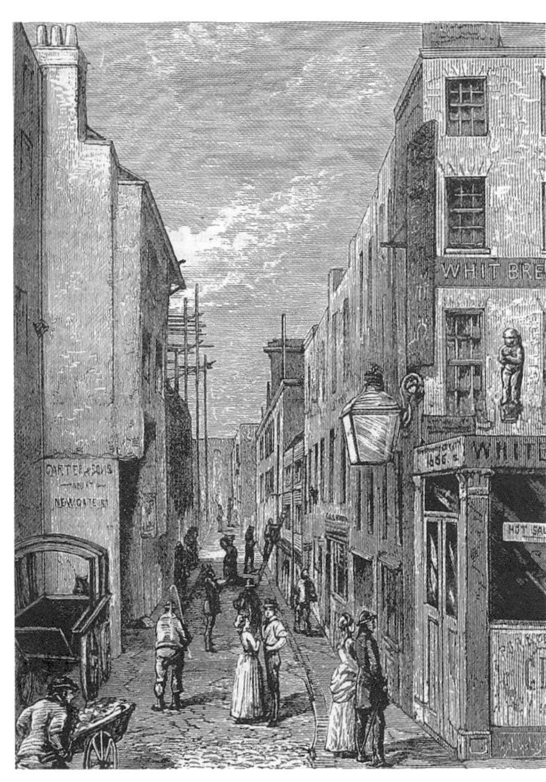

The Fat Boy memorial at Pye Corner.

The Golden Boy as the Fat Boy memorial became.

he entrance to Vauxhall Gardens.

The original Royal Exchange.

Plague doctor, dressed for the part.

His notorious comment about women 'pissing out the fire' was not, in itself, such an absurd notion. The use of urine as a means of extinguishing a fire was recommended when no other liquid was available. It made sense. In a city like London, urine was constantly available; buckets were provided for the collection of waste and in a filthy, rodent-infested warren like the working-class areas of London, nobody was going to be unduly worried by the smell of stale body waste.

In his 1727 novel *Gulliver's Travels* the writer Jonathan Swift later calls on his character Gulliver to urinate on burgeoning flames in order to put out a fire in the tiny town of Lilliput. As Gulliver is a giant with a full bladder, at least in comparison to the miniscule Lilliputians, the fire is swiftly extinguished. Bludworth, if he had been alive, would have been pleased to note that Gulliver was then charged for urinating in public.

Swift's intention was to satirise the human condition and the state of human existence. The passage has since been edited out of most editions of *Gulliver's Travels*, which is now marketed mainly to children. When it was written, the satire was hard-hitting and, as with so much of Swift's work, clearly related to events and incidents that the country's reading public would remember only too well.

Thomas Bludworth was undoubtedly a 'silly man', to use the words of Samuel Pepys. Indecisive and self-indulgent, he was conscious of his own position and the likely consequences for him should he take the one step which would have halted the fire before it had time to spread and destroy so much of the city.

That step was the creation of fire gaps ahead of the flames, something that could be achieved only by pulling down houses in the path of the fire. The flames would have nowhere to go and would eventually burn themselves out.

The tactic did not make allowance for Flash Over where, once the temperature of the air had reached a crucial point, flames would leap across gaps, setting fire to houses that lay some distance ahead. The key was to get in first, destroy properties and create fire gaps at an early stage of the conflagration before the air temperature rose. Early action might have saved many properties, and probably would have done, but this was an action the Lord Mayor totally failed to set in motion.

Alerted and called by the watchmen, he arrived in Pudding Lane promptly enough but refused to listen to advice, either from the locals or from men more experienced than him in fighting fires. If he ordered the pulling down of houses, he argued, then the Corporation would be responsible for the cost of their rebuilding – possibly even Bludworth himself.

It was not only that. He would have to obtain permission from the owners to destroy houses and as most of the properties now threatened by the fire were rented he, along with Corporation officials, had no idea who actually owned the houses. To make the problem even more complex, permission would also have to be granted by the King.

A dynamic official would have taken the risk and sorted out responsibilities later. Pulling down houses was, really, the only way to go. Not for Sir Thomas Bludworth, however. The easy way out was to diminish the risk by mocking it, hence the throwaway line of a woman being able to 'piss it out'.

Having delivered his line, thus ensuring himself a place in history, Bludworth spun on his heels and went back home. After a few disturbed hours in bed he was back at the scene of the fire just after daybreak. The fire had grown in strength and magnitude but swift action might still have saved the day. But not with Thomas Bludworth in charge.

Pepys, who had been to see the King at Whitehall, searched high and low for Thomas Bludworth. He was bustled and battered by the crowds of fleeing citizens but at last he met Bludworth in Cannon Street. It was not the most fortuitous of encounters.

Almost as soon as they met in the crowded street, the mayor became defensive. Criticism from Samuel Pepys, now apparently carrying messages from the King, was the last thing he needed. He began to come out with what was, possibly, the only tactic that might have saved his reputation. He started to lie:

> At last met my Lord Mayor in Cannon Streete, like a man spent, with a handkerchief around his neck. To the King's message, he cried like a fainting woman, "Lord, what can I do? I am spent. The people will not obey me. I have been pulling down houses. But the fire overtakes us faster than we can do it." For himself he must go and refresh himself, having been up all night. So he left me, and I him.[6]

It was all a complete pack of lies. And Pepys, like most people, saw it as such. Bludworth had been at home for most of the night, trying to sleep. He had certainly not pulled down houses or created fire breaks. And the people not obeying him? They probably would have done – if he had issued any commands in the first place.

The next sighting of the Lord Mayor came when the fire was almost out. He was seen directing workers in Cripplegate – another ruse. The danger was virtually over and Bludworth obviously felt secure enough to venture out once more.

By this stage, control of the firefighting lay in the hands of the Duke of York, the Earl of Clarendon and other noblemen. Bludworth had been frozen out of the picture. Even so, gangs of thugs continued to roam the streets searching for victims. They were looking for easy targets, foreigners to assault, refugees to rob. They had begun their vicious work as ad hoc groups, flung together by chance. Soon they became better organised, as if sensing that their period of plenty would be short-lived.

Thanks largely to the insistence of sailors who had come ashore to offer what help they could, the creation of fire breaks had begun, in this case not using hooks to pull down buildings or other traditional methods but by blowing up buildings with dynamite from the Tower of London and the ships in the Thames.

In the months before the fire Pepys and Bludworth had already clashed over the press-ganging of Londoners to fill vacancies in the ships of the Royal Navy. The argument led Pepys to conclude that

Bludworth was a man of mean understanding, poor at his job and totally unsuited to his position as Lord Mayor.

Bludworth's performance during the Great Fire only confirmed the opinion of Samuel Pepys. As time went on others were quick to agree with him.

Pepys's reputation as a recorder of history and social endurance became so vast, so well accepted, that his view of Bludworth was soon being seen as the most accurate account of what went on in those four days in 1666. As he later wrote: 'People do all the world over cry out of the simplicity of my Lord Mayor in general, and more particularly in this business of the fire, laying it all upon him.'[7]

Bludworth had neither the wit nor the skill to respond. He increasingly found himself criticised for spending more time drinking and roistering around the city than in carrying out his duties. His only defence was that he had been Lord Mayor in a year that was brutal beyond belief. His tenure as Lord Mayor ended in October 1666 and the majority of Londoners were more than happy to see him go. He died, largely un-mourned, in May 1682.

* * *

And so to heroes! At the top of the tree, the two men that almost every citizen of London now set high on a pedestal, were King Charles and his brother James, Duke of York. This sudden change of attitude towards the two most visible members of the royal family initially took everyone by surprise.

Being very much a republican enclave, the citizens of London had not held the restored royal family in any degree of esteem or respect. They had accepted the return of the monarchy, some more grudgingly than others, but Charles's subsequent behaviour, wild and self-interested, had offended many of the more puritanical elements in society. It was the same with the Duke of York, but James had the added disadvantage of being a Catholic.

Now, however, they had both responded to the Great Fire in the only way they knew, with courage and determination. Both men were regularly seen in the forefront of the battle to save the city, hauling buckets, smashing down burning timber, carrying out manual tasks from which many men of lower rank and persuasion would have shrunk away.

The trained bands of the city, some 10,000 men, along with the voluntary members of the Artillery Company and military regiments from Tower Hamlets and the city of Westminster, might have borne the brunt of the action but it was Charles and James to whom everyone looked and admired. 'The King, the King!' was the shout whenever anyone recognised the soot-coated monarch and his brother: 'It is not indeed imaginable how extraordinary the vigilance and activity of the King and Duke was, even labouring in person and being present, to command, order, reward and encourage workmen; by which he [the King] shewed his affection to his people and gained theirs.'[8]

Charles was unable to be as hands on as he would have wished, having other responsibilities and duties to occupy him, but he did the next best thing – he appointed his brother to take charge of all firefighting activities. Technically it was a job that should have occupied the Lord Mayor but now Charles simply cut Bludworth out of the equation.

James had always been at his best when he was active. As a soldier and as an admiral he had excelled, and now he threw himself into this new task he had been given. Wherever there was danger, whenever his guiding hand was required, he was present. As a result, all of the approbation and love that should have been directed at the Lord Mayor went, instead, to the two royal brothers.

Inevitably, James called on as many noble friends and acquaintances as he could muster, men he knew he could trust to carry out his orders. The Lords Craven, Manchester, Ashley, Belasyse and Harrison, Privy Councillors all, became his lieutenants. However, the man who caught much of the crowd's attention was the eighteen year old James Scott, Duke of Monmouth.

In command of a company of Life Guards, Monmouth – recently acknowledged as the illegitimate son of King Charles – not only fought the blaze but used his troops to keep order in the streets. In 1685 Monmouth was to rebel against his uncle when James became King, denouncing James's Catholic faith and even accusing him of starting the fire himself.

Defeated at the Battle of Sedgemore, Monmouth's final words before his execution were: 'Prithee, let me feel the axe, I fear it is not sharp enough.' He was right. It took executioner Jack Ketch six strokes to cut his head from his body. In 1666, however, rebellion was the last thing on his mind and the Duke of Monmouth was another significant hero in the eyes of Londoners.

There is another interesting connection between the Duke of Monmouth and the Great Fire. Judge Jeffries, the famous 'hanging judge' who sent over 300 of Monmouth's followers to the gallows in the wake of Sedgemoor, was married to none other than the daughter of the ex-Lord Mayor of London, Thomas Bludworth. There were undoubtedly many in the city of London who wished that Bludworth could have been added to the role of dishonour of the 'hanging judge.'

Heroes abounded throughout the five days of fire. That was inevitable in a disaster of this magnitude. Most of them were known figures, known in appearance, known in power and simply known from the importance of their names. The royals were classic examples of this, understood and, as the fight against the fire continued, appreciated, possibly even loved.

It is hard to be certain, but Charles and James seem to have been driven by emotion and a desire to help rather than by simply aiming to reinforce their status and positions. However you look at it, their significance cannot be underplayed.

There were others, many of them now nameless and all but forgotten. The sailors who had been insisting for some time on the use of gunpowder to create larger and quicker fire breaks are appreciated as a group but their individual names are long forgotten. To them the city owed an immense debt of gratitude.

Admiral Sir William Penn was a member of the Admiralty Board, one of the few sailors whose name we do know. A neighbour and friend of Samuel Pepys, he took control of the 'fire breaking sailors,' directing them from one location to the next, sending them where their help was most required.

Penn is best remembered, however, as Pepys's companion in walking the burning streets and for digging holes in the garden! Having seen others do the same, Penn and Pepys took time to bury and secure their valuable possessions, including Pepys's wine and Parmesan cheese.

Pepys, never one to hide his contribution to the defeat of the fire, made sure that his part in the decision to blow up houses was well recorded and known. His main aim in what happened next was to save his house and the Navy Office but he kept somewhat quiet about that. In his diary entry for Tuesday 4 September, he wrote:

> This afternoon, sitting melancholy with Sir W Penn in our garden and thinking of the certain burning of this office without extraordinary means, I did propose for the sending up of all our workmen from Woolwich and Deptford yards … and to write to Sir W Coventry to have the Duke of York's permission to pull down houses rather than lose this office.[9]

Regardless of whose idea it was, Penn immediately set off for Deptford, some four miles to the east of burning London. There, in the dockyard and naval yard, he ordered parties of sailors and workmen to drop their routine tasks and head off into the city.

The involvement of these men, sailors and dockyard workers alike, was crucial. Along with the change in wind direction, it was probably the most significant factor in defeating the flames. The tragedy is that so few of them are remembered as individuals. Pepys was at least gracious in giving Penn some of the credit in saving the burning metropolis:

> Home, and whereas I expected to have seen our house on fire, it was not. But to the Fyre and there find greater hopes than I expected; for my confidence of finding our office on fire was such that I durst not ask anybody how it was with us, till I came and saw it not burned. I find, by the blowing up of houses and the great help given by the workmen out of the King's yards, sent up by Sir W Penn, there is a good stop to it all.[10]

Other heroes, one named, one not, included the sailor Richard Rower and an unknown or, at least, un-named soldier. On Wednesday evening the pair climbed onto the roof of the Inner Temple and, together, managed to beat out the flames.

The action of the two men saved the building and Rower was rewarded with a gift of £10 from the lawyers and inmates of the Temple. His assistant, the soldier, was presented with a sum of just £2 although why there was a discrepancy between the two rewards is not known.

The escapade was also commemorated in a particularly excruciating example of bad verse written soon after the event by John Crouch. If ever there was a case of distance between event and commemoration being of crucial importance, it is this piece of verse.

Although the poem itself is dreadful, with an adherence to scansion and syllable count to the detriment of pace and product, its main failure comes, yet again, in the fact that it features the sailor rather than the soldier:

> Must she be mow'd down by a sudden death,
> Three days undo a thousand years? Oh yes.[11]

After that reasonable opening, where iambic pentameters create a regular and insistent beat, the poem drops into a mundane search for forced rhyme:

But a brave seaman up the tiles did skip
As nimbly as the cordage of a ship.
Bestrides the sing'd Hall on its highest ridge
Moving as if he were on London Bridge.[12]

And there is still no mention of the anonymous soldier! Fame and heroic status, it seems, do not always have to be attributed – and fortune often goes to those who least expect it.

* * *

Heroes and villains come in many forms. Arguably, the real hero of the hour was the changing wind. Nothing could have stopped the fire if the easterly wind had continued to blow. Yet that same wind had been the original villain. After all, no wind from the east, no fire in the city, no Great Fire of London.

We tend to attribute the blowing up of houses and the creation of fire breaks to Charles and James but there were examples of private individuals doing exactly the same thing. John Vandermarsh, a London merchant of Dutch descent, and a baker called John Gaze both paid labourers to pull down houses of which they were tenants. Their breaks effectively stopped the fires in their districts. Heroes, albeit unacclaimed ones.

Chapter 8

Surveying the Damage

In hindsight, once the brunt of the fire had been dealt with, it was clear to everyone that the damage to London was significant. Wooden buildings with thatched roofs and wattle and daub walls could hardly be expected to survive such an onslaught.

The fire need not have been so destructive if Sir Thomas Bludworth had acted as he should have done. Intervention in the early stages of the outbreak might have helped curtail the fire but the longer Bludworth and the others waited, the more impossible the task became.

Bludworth needed to act with urgency and ruthlessness but those seemed to be words totally unknown to the Lord Mayor. He did not act as he should have done, the fire spread and we must resign that fact to history.

Though the main fire was extinguished by Thursday nightfall there was still fear that it might erupt again. St Paul's Cathedral was, apparently, still alight for most of the day, the flames burning until Friday and not being properly extinguished for several more weeks. Other significant buildings were smoking ruins. If the wind should change direction once more, or if the much-hated Dutch/French/Catholics should seize the opportunity to strike, there would be chaos and confusion once again.

Fear was infectious. Towns all over England were ordered to take steps to defend themselves should the enemy approach. The various militia brigades were called to arms and innkeepers in coastal districts were forbidden to admit into their houses or give lodgings to people they did not know or recognise. Such scaremongering did not last long but while it did it offered a terrifying prospect for the people of England.

With nearly 15,000 houses across the eastern part of London destroyed, almost four fifths of the city, and most of the population now squatting in temporary, makeshift camps on the outskirts, it was inevitable that Londoners should look for people to blame for the disaster.

The baker Thomas Farriner, owner of the house and bakery where the fire had begun, was clear that he was not going to become a victim. He was vocal in his protestations, adamant that he had put everything in order before going to bed on the Sunday night when the fire began. As a juror in Hubert's trial, Farriner made sure that his name was in a prominent position on the Bill condemning Hubert to death for starting the fire.

It is possible that Farriner had a previous criminal record for minor offences. Even so, people believed implicitly in Farriner's version of events. Up to a point what he said was true. A little while later a plaque was even placed on the site of his bakery, seemingly absolving him of all blame:

> Here by permission of heaven, hell broke loose upon this Protestant City from the malicious Hearts of barbarous Papists, by ye hand of their agent, Hubert who confessed and on ye ruins of this place declared the fact, for which he was hanged. Here began that dreadful fire, which is described and perpetuated on and by the neighbouring pillar.[1]

The pillar referred to on the plaque was the enormous monument built to commemorate the disaster, blaming Catholics for starting the fire. Arson by foreign powers continued to be the most popular target for people's anger.

King Charles and his brother James were well aware of the rumours of foreign invasion that were sweeping the refugee camps. Just after mid-day on Thursday 6 September the King, pragmatic to the last, rode to Moorfields where he addressed those refugees who had successfully fled from the blaze. Charles was accompanied only by a few of his courtiers and by a small body of Life Guards: 'He told the people that the fire had been caused by the hand of God and not by any Popish Plot, nor by the French or the Dutch. It was an accident, no more.'[2]

He had interviewed several supposed arsonists, Charles declared, and found no proof that any outside agency had been involved. Those foreigners who had made their homes in the city were as pleased with the King's judgement as any natural-born Englishmen.

Charles finished with a great rallying cry – if the Dutch or French invaded, he would fight and, if necessary, die alongside his subjects. The people, already newly enthralled and given heart by the actions of their King during the fire, believed him.

No-one doubted that he would be alongside them if they had to fight. A new rumour began to spread. There had already been a battle against the French and the Dutch, won by the forces of the King, inflicting 30,000 casualties on the enemy. That, at least, was less worrying than the previous invasion scare.

* * *

Despite the success of the enlarged fire breaks, employed for the first time by officialdom on the Wednesday, the progress of the fire had been relentless. Those citizens still abroad in the ruins late on Thursday evening of the 'fire week' could see that the London they had known and loved had been virtually destroyed. The 'Queen of cities,' as writers like John Crouch described it, was now no more than a collection of broken dreams, smouldering rubble and once proud buildings.[3]

With the dying of the flames, many of the burned-out buildings had collapsed into the narrow streets, making them more impassable than ever. Those that remained erect stood like blackened, half-completed sculptures alongside the roadways.

People wandered amongst the smouldering buildings, picking at rubbish and what might have once been valued personal possessions.

Now they lay abandoned by the refugees and terrified survivors who had fled outside the city walls. Abandoned goods were fair pickings for everyone, from criminals to those looking for mementoes of the fire. A strange, almost ethereal silence shrouded the ruins.

Strangely, despite the silence, there were people everywhere. In fact, the devastated city had become something of a draw for eager and interested tourists. Most of those flocked in from the surrounding districts but there were also visitors from further afield.

Regardless of government advice to stay away, dozens of eager sightseers came to experience the burned-out remains of buildings and maybe even catch a glimpse of a dead body or two. The blackened shell of St Paul's was of particular interest, being visited and enjoyed more now than it ever had been before.

The books, papers and editorial material of the booksellers from Paternoster Row, stored in the vaults below St Paul's, continued to smoulder for up to a week after the fire ended. It was estimated that their destruction eventually cost the booksellers and publishers somewhere in the region of £150,000 to £200,000. Very few businesses could withstand such a claim on their capital with the result that many publishers duly went bankrupt.

The literary trade recovered but it took time. The novel gradually became an accepted format for writers, John Bunyan's *Pilgrim's Progress* and Henry Fielding with *Tom Jones* leading the way. Dryden, Pope and Milton (*Paradise Lost* coming out the year after the fire) were the leaders as far as poetry was concerned. Libraries began to be founded in great numbers, people like John Evelyn collecting over 5,000 volumes for his personal enjoyment.

Evelyn made the journey from Holborn where, as a minor government official, he had been placed in charge of the firefighting position. Now he travelled hopefully into the remains of the city. On his return, he wrote about what he had seen, felt and experienced. What he witnessed soon destroyed any illusions he had:

> I went this morning on foote [sic] from Whitehall as far as London Bridge, thro the late Fleet Street, Ludgate Hill, by St Paul's, Cheapside, Exchange, Bishopsgate, Aldersgate and out to Moorfields, thence thro Cornhill, with extraordinary difficulty, clambering over mountains of yet smoking rubbish and frequently mistaking where I was, the ground under my feete [sic] so hot, as made me not only sweate [sic], but even burned the soles of my shoes.[4]

The Tower of London and its vast supply of gunpowder had survived but many of the other pieces of architectural excellence had not. The list is almost endless – Inner Temple, the Royal Exchange, Guildhall, St Paul's Cathedral and so on. Bricks and mortar, it seemed, did not guarantee survival. As Evelyn wrote in his tortured, half modern, half medieval script, St Paul's was nothing but 'a sad ruin', a once proud and cavernous building that gave Londoners and visitors such great pride: 'Now rent in pieces, flakes of vast stone split in sunder and nothing remaining intire [sic] but the Inscription in the Architrave which, shewing by whom it was built, had not one letter of it defac'd [sic] which I could not but take notice of.'[5]

The River Thames, lifeblood of the community, was a sorry sight. The river and its banks were half full of clothing, pieces of furniture and so much more. Books and papers, the discarded and unwanted product of the city shops and offices, simply added to the feelings of depression and sadness.

The muddy river, full of discarded items, should have offered easy pickings for the criminal elements of the city. It did not, the discarded possessions lying soaked and rotting in the river and on its banks for weeks to come. The neglect had little to do with compassion on the part of the thieves. Quite simply, there were better pickings in the streets and abandoned houses of the city.

While stressing the welcoming attitude of Londoners, one post-fire 'guide book' for the metropolis, written and published some years after the Great Fire, went out of its way to draw the attention of visitors to what was considered a major problem:

> One of the most dangerous class of swindlers are those pretended porters or clerks, who attend about doors or inns, at the time coaches are unloading; or who watch the arrival of post chaises at the doors of the coffee houses. These fellows, by various artifices, frequently obtain possession of the luggage of a traveller, who has occasion to lament his want of suspicion in the loss of clothes and other effects.[6]

Clearly London criminals had learned lessons from the plunderers of the Great Fire, men and women who had developed the crime of pilfering goods and items of value to a fine art.

Not content to leave it there, the writer then went on warn visitors about the prevalence of pickpockets, advising travellers to keep their hands close to their coat pockets or, better still, to not carry money, jewellery and watches at all.

The passing on of bad money in exchange for good was also listed as a 'popular' crime. The art of taking money for the sale of an object and then giving back forged change had grown in strength.

It was all too easy, declared the writer, for peddlers, shop owners or stall holders to pass over false money and then head off to another location before the customers realised they had been conned.

There had undoubtedly been crime before the Great Fire but the advent of disaster and the potential for losing everything seemed to have been a watershed.

The real tragedy, however, lay not in thievery or in the passing of fraudulent coins but in the changes to the city. In particular, there was the sad view of the River Thames. Where houses, offices, warehouses and public buildings had once blocked the view of the river from the north, the vista was now wide open. It was different and the view became, temporarily, a memorial to the disaster.

Samuel Pepys, who climbed once more to a vantage point in the Tower of London to gaze out over the city and the river, called it 'the saddest sight I ever saw'. Considering the sights he had seen and encountered over the past two or three days this was a powerful statement.

* * *

Visitors and tourists, writers and journalists, thrill seekers all of them, might have been hoping to see the corpses of dead men, women and children. If so, they were unlucky and this ghoulish ambition was contained and eliminated at source.

John Evelyn later referred to the stench of dead bodies as he walked through London but he was talking about the remains of people who had died from infection and disease in the days and weeks after the fire finally died away. Visitors who went searching for corpses found virtually nothing of interest to them.

Evelyn may have been circumspect but other writers were a little more exaggerated in their efforts. The Spanish Ambassador reported that over 8,000 people had died in the aftermath and as a result of the fire, most of them whilst trying to recover lost possessions. They were, he said, buried far sooner than they ever expected, by falls of soot, dust and ashes.

Even if only partially correct, 8,000 seems a huge amount when placed alongside the six official deaths accounted for during the fire: 'Five others were killed shortly after the fire by falling masonry and timber while looking for salvage amongst the ruins. But the greatest number of deaths, although how great we not know, were due to exposure.'[7]

When looking at the damage caused, the most significant factor had to be the number of citizens made homeless by the blaze. It is generally supposed that over 100,000, in other words one sixth of the city's population, were rendered homeless by the fire. That included the convicts in the city prisons, every gaol being left virtually uninhabitable.

The official crime statistics showed that there had been, initially, a dramatic drop in offences but statistics and reality are often beasts of very different natures.

The enforced amnesty for minor offences like pilfering hid the fact that as long as the fire raged, and in the days immediately afterwards, crime actually grew in frequency and intensity. That included minor offences along with more serious crimes that pushed at the boundaries of society. The huge numbers of newly escaped, hardened offenders made this an inevitability.

Once the prison walls came down – literally and metaphorically – it was inevitable that the prisoners would make breaks for freedom. With every man and woman needed to fight the fire, little effort was made to recapture them. Consequently, crime figures began to soar.

Robbery and assault, even murder, became almost regular occurrences, with the criminals hiding out in the cellars of abandoned buildings. Postmaster James Hickes was scathing in his assessment of the situation: 'There are many people found murdered ... When they catch a man single [they] whip him, knock him down, strip him from top to toe, blow out their links and leave the man for dead ... no person dare, after the close of evening, pass the streets among ruins.'[8]

Hickes was probably exaggerating when he declared that many people were 'found murdered'. Even so, it was clear to those in authority that an analysis of the damage and a plan for rebuilding the city was urgently needed.

Hickes was hardly a hero but he did fulfil an important role in the days after the blazing buildings were demolished and the fire extinguished. The slow process of rebuilding the city required men and women of integrity and determination. James Hickes was certainly one of these.

He had fled the city with his family when the post office in Threadneedle Street was burned in the early stages of the disaster. However, he returned the following day to set up a temporary post office in the Golden Lion Inn. It meant that the postal services could continue, more slowly than had previously been the case but still a service of sorts.

Despite being burned out of its base, *The London Gazette*, the city's only newspaper at the time, missed only one edition during the fire. Within a week the paper was in back in print, remarking on the lamentable reason for its recent absence:

> The ordinary course of this paper having been interrupted by a Sad and Lamentable Accident of Fire lately in the city of London: It hath been thought fit for the satisfying of minds of so many of His Majesty's good Subjects, whose great needs be concerned for the life of so great an Accident, to give this short but true Account of it.[9]

Employing the services of the Book Women of the city was an astute move. The Book Women were under-paid and under-appreciated, women who worked as street vendors and hawkers, delivering and selling the paper to residents and visitors alike.

Realising the value of these women helped both the paper and the Book Women. James Hickes, along with the paper's owners and managers, was involved in ensuring that a regular supply of news and gossip was available to anyone who required it. The Book Women were never paid their true worth but distributing the paper provided a regular income of a sort.

The Book Women or Book Ladies were an integral but rarely recognised part of Stuart society. Journalists and editors might write the facts, but the Book Women ensured that those facts ended up where they were intended to go – into the hands of the people of London.

Although they were active during the fire, the rebuilding of London and the coming problems of the Jacobite invasions that would take place in the early eighteenth century were the real tests for the Book Women.

As well as selling newspapers and passing on information verbally – for those who could not read – the Book Women also carried and distributed booklets of a somewhat dubious or dangerous nature.

These booklets or chap books were simply anti-establishment diatribes, reading material that was regarded as scurrilous, even treasonous. In a more enlightened age such books would have been welcomed and discussed in open forum. In the seventeenth century they would have led to imprisonment, possibly even the death sentence.

Samuel Pepys was impressed by one of these outlawed chap books. After reading one of them, a pamphlet called *A Catholique Apology*, which had been presented to him by Mrs Michell, his Book Lady, he was moved to comment favourably on its presentation and content.

Praise from Pepys was a rare commodity but this time he was genuine enough in his content. He called this small volume 'a much looked after service, very well writ'.[10]

* * *

On 19 September the King appointed Wenceslas Hollar to survey the devastated city and report back on the damage.

A citizen of Prague, Hollar was assisted by Francis Sandford, author of A Genealogical History of the King's of England. Together they produced one of many reports on the state of London and its likely future. Hollar also drew a plan of the city, showing the areas that had been destroyed as well as those parts that had been left untouched.

The immediate problem was obviously the large number of homeless people in the city and the number of houses that had been destroyed. Estimating the figure of fallen houses at around 15,000, Hollar and Sandford were amazingly accurate.

However, the work of Hollar and Sandford was not so well appreciated when they suggested that the onus for rebuilding should rest with the owners and tenants of the various properties. Given fourteen days to make a response, it was hardly surprising when very few householders bothered to reply. In the end the task was given to contractors.

With between 65,000 and 70,000 Londoners now homeless and a constantly adjusted upwards figure of over £10 million worth of damage, rebuilding London was going to be a major task.

Chapter 9

Post Debacle Efforts – Remembering the Fire

With the frenetic days of the Great Fire finally over, there was something of a lull in the activities of most Londoners. They were exhausted, worn out by the practical side of the affair. These tasks involved blowing up houses, beating at the flames, moving property from one base to another and many other physical activities that were exhausting but which had undoubtedly saved lives.

The psychological effect was different. Emotionally, many of the survivors were distraught and were to remain so for a considerable time. It did not matter how close they had come to death, they had lost nearly all they possessed – houses, furniture, rare items of sentimental value and so on. The citizens, as with the victims of most major disasters, needed cheering up and, to go with it, their city also required considerable cleaning up. Hard and heavy work lay ahead.

Almost immediately it became clear that the more elegant and erudite forms of public entertainment would take weeks, months, maybe even years, to recover and organise. So, how to keep the public happy? 'Quick and cheap' was the obvious motif.

Londoners, like most other natives of the British Isles, were normally well catered for with numerous examples of free or cheap events. May Day dancing, along with its accompanying heavy drinking bouts, circus performances and rowdy fairs where everyone could let their hair down, were a staple diet in towns, villages and cities at the time. They had always been popular in London where, importantly, such entertainments were also available to both men and women.

Fairs and dances? These were the obvious places to begin looking for accessible entertainment but, unfortunately, there was a drawback. Most of the fairs were irrevocably tied to a set time of the year. Even if they could be moved to other dates, star performers like the hugely popular acrobat and tightrope walker Jacob Hall already had their programmes mapped out for months ahead and were unwilling to make alterations.

It was a conundrum that puzzled the King, the aldermen, and councillors of the city when they turned their minds towards entertaining the populace. And, from the beginning it proved to be an insurmountable problem. Attempts to change dates met a brick wall of opposition.

The famous St Bartholomew's Fair, for example, was held every year in August on the Eve of St Bartholomew's Day. The charter for its existence had been granted by King Henry I in 1133, detailing the time of year when it would be held. The 1666 fair had already taken place just a few weeks before the fire, something that took it well out of the reckoning.

It was a similar story with May Day celebrations, where dancing around the Maypole created what were often renowned as wild and unchecked affairs. It would have been ideal but the drawback to the activity could be found in its name, May Day. Such events could only be held in spring.

Consequently, it was soon decided that fairs, visiting circuses and other similar entertainments were useful but they were limited as far as planned enjoyments were concerned. 'Use them when their time approached' – that had to be the governing catch phrase.

Theatre had been popular since the Tudor period when writers like Shakespeare and Kit Marlowe produced plays which appealed both to nobles and to the lower orders. The coming of James, the first Stuart king, saw a sudden advent of masques and miracle plays, old medieval community plays, usually held in the church yard or doorway. These short, undemanding offerings were a change in direction for the playhouses but like theatre in general, they provided entertainment that ordinary people could enjoy. That was until the Puritan restrictions of 1642.

Most theatres found themselves closed down during the Commonwealth period but the Restoration of the monarchy in 1660 saw the return of the playhouses. Almost without effort, theatre became a hugely popular entertainment once again, the advent of women actors like Nell Gwyn and Elizabeth Barry being a particularly welcome development.

In general London's Great Fire of 1666 did not cause too much damage to the theatres, which were situated outside the range of the flames. There were exceptions though. Shakespeare's original Globe had been destroyed in 1613, a second playhouse on the same site being closed by the Puritans in 1642. It was finally destroyed by fire although its fame and connection with Shakespeare ensured that it was never forgotten.

In the months after the fire, other theatres quickly threw open their doors and were well used by the groundlings. Men and women, happy to stand as the actors strove to entertain, made regular use of the playhouses. Such was the popularity of theatre that the years ahead saw several new venues burst into life. These included places such as the Dorset Garden Theatre, which began to operate in 1671, and the Theatre Royal, Drury Lane, which was opened the following year.

Most men, however, preferred a more basic form of enjoyment. Cock Lane, set in one of the seedier sections of the city, was well named. Along with Southwark across the river, it was one of the few city districts where brothels were legal. A few quarts of ale and an hour or two in their favourite 'house of ill repute' would set up many men for the working week ahead or ease the strain of what had gone on in the days before.

Brothels were not government or Corporation-run establishments but in the months after the fire the laws gave them a clear sense of legality. Turning a blind eye to some of the worst repercussions of these legal brothels – syphilis, gonorrhoea, violent altercations between customers, broken marriages and broken heads – meant that the authorities could convince themselves they were going some way to cheering up the hurt and damaged citizens of the capital.

For slightly more decorous and sedate citizens, even if only slightly more sedate, there were also the delights of Vauxhall Gardens, or New Spring Gardens as the complex was originally known. Situated on the south bank of the Thames in the borough of Lambeth, access was by rowing boat until the Vauxhall Bridge was built early in the nineteenth century.

Difficult as it was to actually get there, entrance to the gardens was free. Food and drink were offered for sale in the pleasure groves of the gardens, meaning that the elegant and lamp-lit walkways were rarely as quiet or dignified as the designers had intended. Darkness, solitude, groves of isolation? What more could amorous couples demand?[1]

The New Spring Gardens had actually opened for public use just prior to the Restoration, in the declining years of the Commonwealth. Oliver Cromwell's successor, his son Richard or 'Tumble Down Dick' as he was known, had neither the desire nor the inclination to close the gardens. As a result, it was already a well-used site when social life in the city changed in style and quality. After the Great Fire, the gardens became an even more popular venue for relaxation.

The owners – one of them rumoured to be a relative of Guy Fawkes, of Gunpowder Plot fame – were able to recognise a good thing when they saw it, and more attractions were clearly needed in order to keep the money rolling in. The dark and shielding places of seclusion were still there but the increasing employment of acrobats, jugglers, musicians and fireworks provided the style of entertainment people seemed to want.

The entertainers began the process of turning Vauxhall Gardens, as the resort was soon renamed, into the rumbustious pleasure park it became in the nineteenth century. The writer James Boswell described the area perfectly in his *Life of Samuel Johnson*: 'A mixture of curious show … gay exhibition, musick, [sic] vocal and instrumental, not too refined for the general ear.'[2]

Alcohol was always an essential part of seventeenth-century relaxation and pre-fire London was awash with ale houses, inns and taverns. Many of them were destroyed by the fire but, post-fire, there were enough left to provide solace for the residents of the city.

Amongst those inns and taverns lost to the flames were The Star Inn, adjacent to Farriner's bakery in Pudding Lane. A renowned coach house, it was a relatively new building but was hugely popular with travellers and locals alike.

Notable older public drinking houses lost to the fire included the timber framed Three Cranes Tavern, actually the oldest ale house in London. Then, one of the most popular venues, always full and always ringing with noise, there was the highly acclaimed Boar's Head.

Perhaps the most famous 'victim' was The Mermaid in Cheapside, an inn often mentioned by poets and playwrights like John Webster and Ben Jonson. The writer Francis Beaumont summed up its popularity when he declared, 'What times we had there.'

As well as being one of the oldest and most historically important parts of the city, Cheapside was famous for its taverns and inns. Sadly, the Great Fire put paid to many of them.

That still left plenty of alternative venues. Safe and ready for business were venues like the Hoop and Grapes at the north-west corner of the area affected by the blaze. The Olde Wine Shades, later a popular drinking hole for Charles Dickens and his friends, remained untouched. The tavern even possessed a smuggler's tunnel leading from the main building down to the Thames – although most of the patrons in 1666 were concerned more with what came over the bar than with any historical links to the past.

History struggled in the wake of several of London's public houses. The Staple Inn survived the fire unscathed only to be bombed and destroyed by the Luftwaffe during the Second World War. The Fortune of War was another survivor, going on to become renowned as a place where recently exhumed corpses stolen by the infamous body-snatchers could be held.

And then, of course, for the relatively wealthy people, like Samuel Pepys and John Evelyn, there was always the prospect of drinking at home. Home or public house, the availability of spirits, wine and ale were an essential part of keeping up morale.

For a small body of well-educated individuals, relaxation was to be found in writing. That could be in the form of diary entries, as brought to a fine art by people like John Evelyn and Samuel Pepys, or it could simply be letters, detailing the events and the course of the fire, sent out to relatives and friends. These varied both in quality and regularity.

Henry Griffith did not write while the fire raged but on 18 September he picked up his pen to write to his cousin, also called Henry. He was realistic in his views but, like many of those directly involved, was not always accurate in his recollections: 'the only remedy was conceiv'd to pull down several houses far before the fire, thinking thereby to stop it, but all in vaine [sic] … before one house could be pulled down, ten would have burnt.'[3]

On 3 September John Morgan, a clerk who was always known as Jo, was spending time with friends and colleagues when a near-miss almost ended his life. He was called by his friends to climb to the upper storey of their house in Ffyott Lane in order to see the flames. Squinting through the attic window, they could see that the fire was some distance away from them, seeming to be in the process of destroying Thames Street.

Suddenly a fireball hurled out from the distant flames smashed through the window, narrowly missing Morgan's ear and coming to rest in one corner of the room. Morgan and his friends escaped from the house just before it exploded in a sea of flame.

Like Henry Griffiths before him, Jo Morgan mulled over what had happened, particularly his near miss. Then, when he had things clear in his head, he made a formal witness statement, putting the story down on paper: 'It [the fireball] fell fiercely into the corner of the room and pierced a hole in the boards to the bottom and then, presently, it woosd [sic] up in smoke.'[4]

Official communications were hardly relaxing but they had to be made. Events like the Great Fire were reported, but how they were received depended on a whole range of political rationales. The Venetian Ambassador to France wrote to the Doge of Venice explaining that the French King Louis had taken a somewhat relaxed attitude to the disaster.

An implacable enemy of England, Louis was clear that he would fight his traditional enemy anytime, anywhere. However, according to the Ambassador, his enmity only went so far: 'He would not have any rejoicings about it [the fire], being such a deplorable accident involving injury to so many unhappy people.'[5]

Even so, Louis did go a stage further, offering food supplies to the homeless Londoners. It did not stop him rubbing his hands in glee as, militarily speaking, the fire had been a stroke of luck. Now French ships in the Channel would be free from attack by the Royal Navy, for a while at least.

Meanwhile, public events continued. Wrestling, boxing and tug of war events were quickly arranged. Apart from the excitement of the fighting and gouging between the competitors, the chief interest in attending these events as a spectator was the opportunity to bet on the outcome.

There was also money for the wrestlers and fighters, large purses that many considered worth risking injury to claim. In the first few months after the fire was extinguished, an 'open' wrestling match was arranged with a cash prize of £1,000, an enormous sum of money in the 1660s, being offered to the winning team. It was claimed by a group of fighters from the West Country who had come to London specifically to take part. They defeated another team of travelling competitors, men from the North Country.

The Church, obviously, played a part. On the first Sunday after the extinguishing of the fire, 9 September, thousands crowded into those churches left standing. Open-air services were also held but those who could make the journey from their temporary camps outside the city preferred their local parish churches. Samuel Pepys was one of these: 'Up, and was trimmed, and sent my brother to Woolwich to my wife to dine with her. I to church, where our parson made a melancholy but good sermon – and many, and most in the church cried, especially the women. The church mighty full, but few of fashion, and most strangers.'[6]

For the first time in several weeks, it began to rain that Sunday. Many people took it as God's blessing, thanking them for their efforts and for attending Church service that day. It was the start of a heavy period of rain. For ten days it poured, almost without ceasing. The city needed it but the downpours arrived, arguably, a week too late.

* * *

In the wake of the disaster it became clear that some form of commemoration of the fire and its effects was required. Many of the refugee citizens of London wanted the disaster that had destroyed their homes and lives to be remembered. After all, the fire had been the greatest threat ever known to the city and its population. And yet, while rebuilding the wasted houses and churches was one thing, a tasteful commemoration of the disaster was something else.

The initial response to this way of thinking came in the form of literature, poetry in particular. Much of the Restoration verse, particularly the examples that followed in the wake of the Great Fire, has been long forgotten. The reason for that is simple.

The vast majority of the commemorative verse was not just poor, it was downright bad! The poets had chosen to ignore or had forgotten the old adage, well understood by people like the ancient Greek and Roman writers of the classical world, that good poetry should describe and tap in on 'experience reflected in tranquillity'.

The message was simple enough. Endure or enjoy the experience but wait before committing your thoughts to paper. Shakespeare and Marlowe understood well enough that writing in the heat of the moment, while emotions and feelings were still raw, rarely achieved anything more than banality. The renowned poet William Wordsworth was later to hone the concept to a fine art but for many of the Stuart poets it was a skill and achievement that was never attained.

Put simply, most of the post-fire poetry was produced too soon after the event to be anything more than childlike incantations with poor rhymes and a general lack of poetic technique. Arguably, such writing was a release of emotions. Which is fair enough, but as far as pure poetic technique was concerned, it should have been condemned to the writer's bottom desk drawers and never published.

The offerings were not all bad, however. Perhaps the best remembered verses from this period are traditional nursery rhymes that are still sung and chanted today by young children in the playground and school yard.

These nursery rhymes may well be based on older pieces of writing, poems that were now revamped and brought up to date. This is best seen in lines such as, 'Here comes a chopper to chop off your head,' found in the eternal favourite 'Oranges and Lemons'. That particular rhyme may not refer to the Great Fire at all but instead be a reference to ancient pagan child sacrifices. Whatever its origin it was now, post-1666, that its popularity really began.

The nursery rhymes or chants – and there were dozens of them – were repeatedly sung in the days after the fire. Arguably people, adults and children alike, had no other way of relaxing or entertaining their children, who had been suddenly taken away from everything they knew and understood.

In many cases, the lyrics were so specific that they can only be about the fire and its consequences. 'London's Burning' is a good example of this:

London's burning, London's burning,
Fetch the engine, fetch the engine,
Fire, fire, fire, fire,
Pour on water, pour on water
London's burning, London's burning.[7]

The theme and subject of the rhyme are obvious, commemorating the fire succinctly in that single line – 'London's burning.' It was clearly a poem of the time. The use of repetition effectively hammers home the point of the rhyme – London IS burning. It is a powerful piece of poetry for the very young.

There were several other nursery rhymes about the fire. 'Oranges and Lemons' can be interpreted as the story of the destruction of seven London churches while 'London Bridge is Falling Down' is a commemoration of something that everyone thought was about to happen but which, in the end, was not the case.

Many of the adult poems written as a knee-jerk response were produced immediately after the fire was quelled but not published until much later. Unlike the nursery rhymes, which take an overarching view, the majority of the adult poetry from this period tends to focus on specific events or parts of the disaster. The poem of one writer, F. Wright, takes the destruction of St Paul's and the books under its floors as its opening theme:

> See yet another Ruin: here were laid
> Choice authors, by the servants of the muses.[8]

Thomas Ward set his gaze upon the so-called Popish Plot which, fuelled by the anti-Catholic feelings of the time, followed quickly on the heels of the fire. The verse is as bad as that of any other poet of the era and is also historically incorrect. According to Ward, Titus Oates, the instigator of the Popish Plot, was the man behind setting London on fire:

> In sixteen hundred sixty six
> That they through London took their matches
> And burned the city down with torches[9]

Oates would probably have been glad to be regarded as the instigator of the fire but, sadly for him, he was not.

The glut of bad verse continued for several months after the fire, when time and distance should have given the writers at least a degree of objectivity. As this anonymous and poorly contrived poem shows, there was never going to be a substitute for skill:

> Such was the rise of the prodigious fire
> What in mean buildings first already bred
> From there did soon to open streets aspire
> And so to pleasant temples spread.[10]

It was not all bad, however. Some of the poetry produced in these months almost managed to escape the condemnatory phrase 'bad verse.' Witness the efforts of Samuel Wiseman, a little-known poet who produced one or two pieces that describe the early hours of the fire:

> Horror and fear, and sad distracted cries
> Chide sloth away and bid the sluggard rise.[11]

Wiseman was a rarity. He was the tip of a powerful iceberg and of course there were other exceptions to the canon of bad vcrsc, notably John Dryden and John Milton. As far as skill and talent are concerned, most of the other Restoration poets never came within a hair's breadth of their coat tails. No matter how effective they were, though, the two great writers were hugely different from each other.

Dryden was a man of the Restoration, a Royalist through and through. He was not above being critical of Charles and the regime established after his restoration to the monarchy but in 1667 John Dryden was appointed Poet Laureate, the first person to ever hold the post. Milton was his direct opposite, a staunch Republican, opposed to the Restoration and all the new king stood for. His classic works like *Paradise Lost* and *Samson Agonistes* have earned him a prominent place in the pantheon of poetic greats.

Dryden's *Annus Mirabilis* was, and remains, a majestic piece of work. It is made all the more powerful because it does not just centre on the Great Fire. It covers English victories in the war against the Dutch and the plague of 1665 before actually getting to the fire, which is only dealt with in the second half of the poem. That, in Dryden's imagination, is what makes 1666 a truly memorable year – memorable but hardly glorious.

In *Annus Mirabilis*, one of his most renowned pieces, Dryden takes a personal view, imagining and reflecting how the people of his city are feeling. It is a truly effective poem, even though it is in no way an example of emotion reflected upon at leisure and in tranquillity:

> Night came, but without darkness nor repose,
> A dismal picture of the general doom:
> Where souls, distracted, when the trumpet blows,
> And half unready with their bodies come.[12]

Poetry might have been popular but it hardly had a universal appeal. Many Londoners could not read; for others verse, no matter how good or bad it might be, had an ethereal quality that was beyond them. For people like that a more obvious form of memorial was required.

* * *

A memorial or monument was the answer. It would take time to fund, design and build such a monument and in the end there were actually two commemorative offerings, along with a number of commemorative plaques on places of interest which had a relevance to the fire.

First and foremost, however, the streets needed cleaning. A meeting of the Council of State, held on Monday 10 September, ordered that the citizens must clean and clear the streets and lanes of London. Their houses might have gone but everyone, the Council declared, would be held responsible for clearing their own land.

It was a logical decision. No progress could be made on starting to rebuild houses and other buildings until all of the detritus of the fire had been collected and disposed of, away from danger and possible misuse.

Wood, bricks and stone from collapsed houses lay like carbuncles in the streets. Piled up mounds of smouldering rubbish lay in front of most houses, a potential fire risk that could be kicked into life by any small child or animal. A return to anything resembling normality would only be possible when it was all removed.

At the same time an accurate record needed to be made of what people had lost. That record was particularly important for businessmen, many of whom had not only lost their houses but also their places of business.

Many businessmen survived the fire and its fallout. They picked up the pieces of their livelihood and started again. Others were unable to do so and ended up in one of the city's debtor's prisons. It was 1671, five years after the fire, before an Act of Parliament was passed to release prisoners being held in custody for debt caused by the Great Fire of London.

Regardless of the rain and gloom of that autumn and winter, fires continued to smoulder for a further six months. The temperatures in the streets and houses were high and it was common to see smoke coming from burned-out buildings.

It was not just smouldering remains; occasional outbreaks of blazing fire also sometimes occurred, usually in the cellars of previously untouched houses where papers, books and kindling were stored. Rain might deluge the city but the water often failed to reach the flammable material in the cellars with the result that many of the cellars and storage spaces were little better than tinder boxes, just waiting to be lit.

It was a difficult time, a period that was in many ways as dangerous as the fire itself, and it needed careful handling by the authorities. In the meantime, despite the difficult economics of the time, donations of money to help feed and house the homeless and the destitute were received from a variety of different sources.

Responding to a Royal proclamation from the King, large cities like York and small country parishes such as Marlborough sent donations of money that varied in size according to the donors' financial circumstances. Even tiny Lyme Regis in Dorset submitted a sum of £100.

Further proclamations encouraged a process of 'internal emigration' in an effort to reduce the homeless population of London. Temporary or permanent, anything which reduced the drain on city resources was welcome. It was difficult to refuse help when the monarch requested it in such a forthright manner: 'All cities and Towns whatsoever shall without any contradiction receive the said distressed persons and permit them the free exercise of their manual trades.'[13]

The citizens of Ireland tried to donate herds of cows rather than cash but as the import of cattle into England was forbidden, no donation of any sort was received from the Irish. Individual subscriptions were received, however, from the rich colonists in Ulster.

The contribution from York led to an interesting development. In the wake of the money, King Charles received a message from the citizens of the northern city, suggesting that as London had been so badly burned York should take over as the capital city of the country. After all, York was one of the oldest communities in England, the message read, and had been graced by a number of ancient historic buildings. The King's reply was short, succinct and would not grace either a female audience or the walls of a religious house!

Parliament had not been sitting when the fire broke out, most MPs sitting safe and comfortable back home in their constituencies, but a Council of State was quickly called. The missing members of Parliament returned to the city and the Council of State met for the first time on 10 September. Prominent London citizens and aldermen from the city added to the MPs who now sat in what was effectively the centre of leadership for London.

The meeting took place at Gresham House. For the past six years it had been home to the Royal Society before they were ejected in favour of the Council of State. In the following days and weeks Gresham House became a centre for merchants and businessmen to meet and discuss their trades.

Taking over Gresham House was the first time that any city building had been commandeered for use by the governing body. It was only the start. Other buildings joined Gresham House, providing homes for causes and professions for which they had never been designed. It was a question of 'needs must' in the battered city.

Other temporary arrangements came to include the Customs House, which was set up in the home of Lord Bayning; at the same time, a new Excise Office was established in a large property on Southampton Fields.

The new headquarters of the Post Office was established, first, in Brydges Street before moving to another property in Bishopsgate Street. They were all temporary moves, but their continued efficiency was a tribute to the various work forces.

With most of the members called back for duty in London, Parliament hastily reassembled, meeting for its first session on 18 September. The main point of discussion was, obviously, how to repair and rebuild the city. One of the members' first tasks was to appoint their own committee to investigate the cause of the fire.

As September drew to a close, a Royal Proclamation was issued, forbidding anyone to rebuild their houses. Regulations would soon be issued for a degree of uniformity in any rebuilding. The message was simple, if not always welcomed by the householders – be patient, wait for the order to begin work on your property.

Chapter 10

Remember, Remember the Second of September

The Parliamentary committee called to investigate the causes of the fire met for the first time on 26 September 1666, under the chairmanship of Sir Robert Brooke.

Arguably, for the majority of Londoners the result of the committee's deliberations was a forgone conclusion. It should be, as far as the refugees and the homeless citizens were concerned, easy to see where those in authority could find and then apportion punishment for the four days of destruction.

Among most of the London residents it had already been unofficially agreed, although not proven, that the causes could be found in the frenetic and evil workings of Catholic, French and Dutch brains.

The public's beliefs were clearly a case of wishful thinking, a continuation of the view that took hold during the raging fire. It was the easiest verdict to return and was far more obvious, more fulfilling, than declaring the fire a mere accident. And the early decisions of the Parliamentary committee seemed to be leaning towards that popular viewpoint.

Within a few days of its first meeting, the committee had asked the King to banish all Catholic priests from England. Charles acquiesced and gave the Jesuits and other Catholic religious leaders until December to leave the country. Anti-Catholic feelings and emotions, never exactly hidden, had once more resurfaced.

However, when the formal report was presented by the committee in January 1667 it was not quite what the hardliners had expected. Put simply, the committee chose to prevaricate.

After making the statement that they had given the matter intense scrutiny, the report declared that 'nothing had yet been found to argue it [the fire] to have been other than the hand of God upon us, a great wind and the season so very dry'.[1]

The decision was accepted by government but not by the people, who were soon demanding that the committee should sit again and come up with a different conclusion. The London mob was up in arms and for weeks on end people now came forward with new accusations, claiming that they had seen fire bombers at work, hurling explosives through shop and house windows. Always there was Catholic or foreign involvement somewhere in their stories.

Nobody was safe. From harmless shoe polishers and street hawkers to solicitors and shop owners, a slip of the tongue or a failure to report comments overheard in the bar room could lead to physical attack and the destruction of property.

Monsieur Belland, the King's Firework Master, soon became a prime target for accusation. He had in his possession, it was claimed, the means and the experience to create a blaze like nobody had ever seen before. As a skilled maker of fireworks, it was not exactly something he could deny.

As public anger swelled and became increasingly vocal, Belland and his family fled. They sought refuge in Whitehall palace where, they assumed, they would be safe. On at least one occasion, however, Belland and his son were confronted by the hunting mob, which had somehow gained access to the palace. Belland managed to escape by threatening the leaders with a lawsuit.

Anti-Catholic feelings spread out far beyond London. In the belief that there was a Catholic plot to destroy many of England's great cities, any foreigner who could not account for his or her movements around the time of the fire was promptly arrested. Foreign sailors, servant girls, merchants and businessmen, all were vulnerable. Most of them, after cooling their heels for some time in the less than comfortable bridewells of the country's court rooms, were released.

The King, his religious beliefs always unclear, was disturbed by the ugly mood of the country but he was helpless to change public opinion. His brother James, an open and avowed Catholic, was a perfect target. He was not alone. Even children as young as ten or eleven were accused of complicity, some of them appearing to be more than happy to shoulder blame:

> The Lord Chief Justice gravely investigated the many suspects brought before him and even took seriously the examination of one Edward Taylor, a ten year old apothecary's boy who swore that his father and uncle had destroyed the city between them … "The boy's age renders the whole suspected," wrote an investigator, "but it is to be put into my Lord Chief Justice's hands."[2]

Most of the accusations from the London mob were ignored by the authorities, Lord Clarendon stating that it was impossible to hear evidence like that of young Edward Taylor without smiling! Inevitably, although temporarily, the violence gradually died away. But the belief that foreign powers, notably those supporting the Papacy, were involved in setting the fire remained simmering for many years.

In fact, anti-Papist views remained almost commonplace until the Titus Oates affair of 1678. Oates, a rabble-rouser of the first order, claimed to have knowledge of a Papal or Popish Plot which had been contrived in 1666 to set fire to the city. He was eventually denounced as a liar and a fraud, and the hard edge of anti-Catholicism perished with him.

It did not go away entirely, however, the Catholicism of the future King James leading to his abdication and exile soon after he came to the throne. It was a far cry from the heady days when James was acclaimed as a hero of the fire. Inevitably, his exile led to the Jacobite rebellions and revolts up to and including the invasion of Bonnie Prince Charlie in 1745.

As late as 1680 Parliament passed a resolution stating that the fire had been started by Papists and it was the middle of the nineteenth century before the truth – accident, pure and simple – was officially acknowledged.

* * *

So, the creation of a large permanent monument to commemorate the fire and the lives lost during and directly after the blaze? It seemed like a good idea and was agreed upon soon after the fire was extinguished. King Charles was active in promoting the scheme, just as he was complicit in the planning of a new city. The actual work, however, would be funded and carried out by the Corporation of London.

A 202-foot Doric column was designed by the architect Sir Christopher Wren, aided by Robert Hooke. It was originally intended that the column should be surmounted by a figure of King Charles II but this idea was quickly dropped in favour of a brass urn. Flames would emerge from each side of the urn, helping to make the column and memorial hugely effective.

The column was to be located on the site of the now-demolished St Margaret's church in Fish Hill Street, some 130 feet away from Farriner's Bakery in Pudding Lane.

There was to be a bas-relief on the western side of the monument, showing King Charles protecting his people and offering freedom to its inhabitants. An inscription declaring that the city was rebuilt within three years featured on the relief. It was a mistake or, it has been argued, possibly a deliberate falsehood.

Following the failure of Titus Oates and the Popish Plot in 1678, an addition was made to the memorial. A new message was added to the Monument itself, Lord Mayor Sir Patience Ward writing the following: 'The burning of this Protestant city was begun and carried on by the treachery and malice of the Popish faction, in order to the effecting their horrid plot for the extirpating the Protestant religion and English liberties, and to introduce Popery and heresy.'[3]

The message might have been what the people wanted but it was both incorrect – most of the rebuilding of the city was not completed until 1676 – and far too florid in composition.

The message was removed on the accession of James II, only to be carved once more after the Glorious Revolution brought Protestant Dutchman William of Orange and his wife Mary to the throne. The plaque was finally removed in 1830.

As Lord Mayor, Sir Patience Ward was hardly in the same class as Thomas Bludworth but he was limited in understanding and, like his predecessor, more than a little interested in his own reputation and standing within the city.

The efforts of Patience Ward on the additional plaque caused the publication of an anonymous poem – probably the work of Samuel Garth – which condemned the man, his mission and his additional message:

He his godly masons sent
T'engrave it round the Monument.
They did so; but let such things pass,
His men were fools, and he an ass.[4]

The Monument was opened for public viewing in 1677, eleven years after the decision to erect it was first made.

* * *

The 202-foot-tall Monument in the area of Pudding Lane was not the only commemorative offering from the local authorities in London. Two other examples were produced and are still in existence today.

A plaque at the site of Thomas Farriner's bakery was a simple enough record of how and why the fire began. Its very simplicity makes the plaque far more interesting than it was ever intended to be, even though its message was never totally accurate.

It took the view that Robert Hubert, who confessed to a crime he did not actually commit, was the culprit. Regardless of huge gaps in his story, the jury – which included Thomas Farriner and his son in its number – found him guilty and Hubert was duly hanged for his 'crime.' How Farriner got himself onto the jury remains a matter of conjecture.

One other lasting memorial, that of the Fat Boy, was created at Pye Corner, the westernmost extent of the fire. The Pudding Lane column might mark the area where the fire began but the understated offering at Pye Corner was erected close to the area where it was finally put out.

The Fat Boy was deliberately erected on the corner of Giltspur Street and Cock Lane in Smithfield, Pye Corner as the location was known. It was a regular meeting place for citizens as well as being a well-known drop-off point for coaches arriving in the city. But there was a more subtle intention in the choice of this specific location.

Pye Corner (Pie Corner as it was sometimes written) and Pudding Lane – the names were important to the memorial makers, symbolising the overindulgence of the pre-fire days. The statue of the Fat Boy added to the message.

The Fat Boy statue was originally located in an alcove on the front wall of The Fortunes of War, a public house that survived the fire only to be pulled down as part of redevelopment in 1910. The public house may be gone but the statue survives.

The idea behind the statue of such a prodigiously corpulent youth was to hammer home the fact that this was not about celebrating the human body. Rather, it was emphasising the point that gluttony and overindulgence were, in part, causes of the Great Fire –hence Pye Corner and Pudding Lane!

Made of wood, the Fat Boy statue was, in the nineteenth century, eventually glossed over and gilded. It then took the name of The Golden Boy, the appellation Fat Boy being considered inappropriate and consigned to history.

Formerly graced by a pair of wings, the statue was given a brief inscription – 'Put up for the late Fire of London, Occasioned by the Sin of Gluttony, 1666.'

The causes of the fire were, it seemed, quite clear to the aldermen. On the one hand there was a deranged and would-be arsonist who had maliciously set the fire. On the other side of the coin rested the terrible sin of gluttony. Using Hubert as the instrument, gluttony won the day.

Arguably, the people of London did not really require monuments and plaques. The events of September 1666 were too close to ever be forgotten by those who had lived through the experience.

* * *

If the people of London did somehow manage to put the fire and its consequences to one side, at least until the city could be rebuilt or refashioned, then the blackened ruins of the broken buildings were there to remind them every time they ventured out of doors: 'The glory of London is now fled away like a bird, the trade of London is shattered and broken to pieces.'[5]

People had lost their houses, their possessions, and been hurled out of their routines and structure. For some the losses could be best counted in financial terms. The booksellers and publishers who had stored their manuscripts in St Faith's and St Paul's had been particularly hard hit.

Estimates vary but their losses had to be somewhere in the region of £150,000. It was, as Adrian Tinniswood has written, 'a catastrophe for the history of English publishing'. The publisher John Ogilvy lost his entire stock and was left with just £5 in capital. Other publishers and booksellers suffered a similar disaster.

The real losers, however, were the writers. William Dugdale's new book *Originales Juridiciales* had just come off the presses and this, along with 300 copies of his *History of St Paul's* and all of his manuscript copies, was burned to cinders. He was left with nothing.

It was not just the writers and authors. Illustrators and engravers, whose work was used to highlight the text of various books and periodicals, were equally as hard hit. No monument or stone edifice could replace such a loss.[6]

Similarly, the disaster was not confined simply to esoteric items like books. Many engravings and paintings, some intended as illustrations to the books, others for display and collection, were also lost. The list of suffering professions went on and on. The clothiers, who normally sold their cloth at Blackheath Hall, were hit for approximately £25,000.

Coal and wood, commonly used for cooking and heating, along with many other necessities of life, were in great demand but not readily available, so much having been destroyed during the fire. Rental prices of houses, formerly set at around £40 per annum, had now reached upwards of £150.

Hundreds of householders had been made homeless. Most of these unfortunates had been renting their properties. That did not help their distress and discomfort as the losses were simply passed on to the owners. But rental prices were now astronomical and would remain so until new properties were built.

Everywhere you looked, prices had shot up so that Samuel Pepys was happy to pay £2 for a book that would, in the pre-fire days, have cost him 8 shillings. Pepys was lucky – he could afford it. Many other Londoners could not.

The emotional or psychological cost of the fire remains almost impossible to count. At the time, the emotional damage to a human being after a traumatic event like the Great Fire was a concept that did not feature in the minds of doctors, surgeons and the public in general.

Physical damage, to the body, that they could cope with. But the hidden interior damage, to a person's soul and concept of self, was something that did not even register on the intellect of the medical professionals at that time.

The Monument near Pudding Lane, the Pye Corner statue and the plaque on the site of Farriner's bakery were there for the future, to remind tourists and newcomers to the city about what had happened during those September days and nights.

A National Fast Day to commemorate the men and women who had died during and after the fire was held on 10 October. It was also a day of thanksgiving – although the destruction of property was vast, the loss of life was relatively small.

The day began with the Dean of St Paul's preaching to the King and to the Court. This was quickly followed by the Bishop of Exeter addressing the House of Lords and the Bishop of Worcester preaching to the Commons. Later in the day the Bishop of Gloucester preached to the people.

In their various addresses, all of the clergymen stressed the moral lessons to be learned from the Great Fire. It was also a day to raise money to help with rebuilding and assist in the feeding of the refugees. In all £12,794 was raised during the day. With the 'celebration' over, it was time to turn to more practical matters.

The immediate task, once the streets were cleared of rubbish, was to rebuild the city. As the situation currently stood, the effect on trade was appalling. If nothing was done about the shattered buildings and the infrastructure of England's leading centre of trade and commerce, the situation would only grow worse.

So, rebuild, and do it quickly, was the general consensus of opinion. It was an opinion held by the authorities and citizens alike. Alexander Pope caught the mood of the people and the state of the city in his poem *The Alley*:

> And on the broken pavement, here and there,
> Doth many a stinking sprat and herring lie;
> A brandy and tobacco shop is near,
> And hens and dogs, and hogs, are feeding by.[7]

Pope, satirical and condemnatory as ever, was light years ahead of the authorities but then, he did not have to clear up the problem. The authorities continued to allow refuse and waste to build up in the streets and condoned animals like pigs and cattle wandering past the houses and the refuse dumps. Pope knew the value of rebuilding, saw it as an essential ingredient in the growth of civilised society. So the message in his short but virulent poem was rebuild and rebuild now.

That was easier said than done. Rebuilding the devastated city was something which required skill, audacity and a clear view of what lay in the future. It also required money.

Chapter 11

A New City, A New Concept

Sir Christopher Wren, deputy surveyor of His Majesty's Works, was quick off the mark when it came to presenting a case for the rebuilding or, as he almost certainly saw it, the re-designing of the city of London. He presented his plan to the King on Monday 10 September, just one week after the blaze began.

At this stage many of the original buildings, and the piles of debris outside the places where the houses used to be, were still smouldering. They were occasionally fanned into bright flames by a sudden gust of wind or by a careless boot from a passer-by. Christopher Wren was able to look beyond these ruins, however. He had a vision and a dream of what the new city could and should look like. Nobody could accuse him of sleeping on the job.

Wren's plan involved creating long and straight thoroughfares running across the metropolis from the two main entry points into the city – the Tower in the east and Ludgate in the west. These main arteries would be crossed several times by a number of smaller roads or avenues leading down to the Thames.

John Evelyn was not far behind Wren. Realising that any form of rebuilding would need a man of skill and foresight at the helm, Evelyn's plans were laid in the King's lap just two days after Wren's, on Wednesday 12 September.

Evelyn's document was examined by the King and his brother and discussed in, of all places, the Queen's Bedchamber. The bedchamber was a totally private and confidential environment, the ideal place to debate and not be overheard. Evelyn thought that the King and the Duke of York were pleased with what they saw and read. He was right.

His plans remained a favourite of the King's. Evelyn, however, was upset that Christopher Wren had stolen a march on him and made his mark a few days earlier: 'Dr Wren got a start on me, but both of us did coincide so frequently that His Majesty was not displeased.'[1]

A third competitor soon arrived on the scene. This was Robert Hooke, then Reader of Mathematics at Gresham College and a noted philosopher. Hooke's scheme was simple, involving a grid of straight and rigid roads running east to west. Like Wren's ideas, it was a logical patterned grid system, one that has since been used in the USA and on modern British cities like Milton Keynes.

In quick succession a number of other plans were soon designed and put before the three bodies that would be making the decision. These were logically the three most suitable agencies, being the King and his Court, the Houses of Parliament and their recently appointed committee, and the City of London Corporation. Amongst others, renowned figures like the city surveyor Peter Mills, celebrated cartographer Richard Newcourt and former Parliamentary soldier Captain Valentine Knight all put forward their ideas.

However, when the 'contestants' were shown the plans recently drawn up by Wenceslas Hollar on the orders of the King, the immensity of the damage that had been caused was suddenly apparent. So too was the area left untouched. As a result of viewing the Hollar document many of the would-be city designers decided they needed to redraw their ideas.

John Evelyn went a stage further. Despite the King's approval of his original offering, he revised his offering and produced two new designs.

There were similarities between all of the various plans and designs but one over-riding factor was paramount. Heavily influenced by recent architectural designs from Italy and Germany, each planner saw the fire as an opportunity to revise London's street layout, making it both functional and attractive to look at.

With most of them involving a criss-crossing series of roads, either in part or in totality, many of the ideas suggested a series of rotundas, open spaces from which roads would radiate. Importantly, on virtually all of the suggestions, the streets would be straight as arrows, wide and not over-hung by buildings or old-fashioned jetties. By their very nature the new roadways would preclude another severe fire like the blaze of 1666.

Uniformity of style and building materials were also common factors in the proposals. The King had decreed that brick or stone were to be used rather than wood and straw, with open spaces for recreation set in amongst the new layouts. All proposals were logical and in keeping with the views of King Charles.

However, the one thing they all lacked, including front runners like Wren and Evelyn, was an appreciation of the city's past. If any of them had been accepted as they were, without alteration, the history of London would have been wiped out. That was to be a major factor in the decision-making process.

One of the greatest drawbacks of the schemes proposed by John Evelyn, John Hooke and several others was that they would require streets leading directly to and from the Thames.

That would have meant steep roadways lined by houses that would either stand crookedly on an impossible incline or need shoring up to make them level. They would also have steep gardens which would be almost unworkable for the residents. For that reason, if nothing else, Hooke's scheme in particular was quickly dismissed.

Hooke had garnered a strong set of supporters, including the Lord Mayor and a number of aldermen. His chance of planning and implementing the new city developments might have vanished but his supporters remained loyal and managed to obtain for him the post of City Surveyor.

Most of the other suggestions met with a similar response from one or other of the three judging bodies. Some of the more impractical ones were dismissed out of hand. Others warranted at least some degree of study.

Newcourt's ideas were dismissed as, in the eyes of those carrying out the judgement, they showed little or no understanding of the topography of the city as it had been and would be in the future. To complete his scheme deep ditches or caverns would have to be crossed or filled in and that put the cost at an astronomical level.

His overarching concept of a city built around a large central square, supported by smaller ones, might have worked on flat, open spaces like the Italian plains but not, the Parliamentary committee decided, on the banks of the River Thames.

The problem of finance – or lack of finance – was never far away. Captain Valentine Knight's proposal foundered on the idea of creating a canal for barges running from Billingsgate to the River Fleet. Such a project would involve raising huge sums of money and, as he saw it, the only source for the large sums required was the Crown.

The investment, according to Knight, could be repaid by fines and fees levied on the barges using the canal. The idea was angrily rejected, particularly by the King and his courtiers. The concept of the King benefitting from the Great Fire was anathema to the Crown and to the King's suffering subjects. Knight was publicly rebuked, arrested and held in custody for the temerity of his suggestion.[2]

* * *

It was not just the King and the Crown that provided stumbling blocks. The overarching factor that caused most of the suggestions to fail or be rejected was the simple fact that the land on which the city was situated was owned, not by one party like the Crown but by many different individuals and organisations. Agreement over issues like the rebuilding was unlikely. That was not a problem to be glossed over.

The other significant question was simple – should there be as many houses in the redeveloped, rebuilt city as there had been pre-1666? Everyone of significance, not to mention the tenants of the burned-out houses, agreed that, for many years, London had been over-populated, something that had led inevitably to squalor and terrible living conditions. Arguably, it also led to the Great Fire and the city's own destruction.

One solution was the compulsory purchase of the land, the money to be advanced by the Crown and/or the London Corporation. When the rebuilding was complete the new properties and the land on which they stood would be sold back to the original owners. The scheme was suggested but was rejected by Parliament and was abandoned at an early stage.

Lack of money was, inevitably, the rock on which most of the plans for the future of the city foundered and sank. Samuel Pepys estimated that the losses caused by the fire to traders, merchants, investors, property owners and citizens in general lay somewhere in the region of £600,000. He was amazed that the men and women of London were able to shoulder the burden and carry on with their lives: 'Never so great a loss as this was borne so well by the citizens in the world as this … All men are busy in looking after their own business, to save themselves.'[3]

As far as Pepys was concerned it was a clear case of people dealing with their immediate problems. And, of course, that meant any re-development of the city would have to wait.

In 1666 the Crown and the Corporation were both in parlous financial positions. War with the Dutch and the French was expensive, costing the government a small fortune. The plague of 1665 had caused significant overspend and a decline in income from trade. Now the destruction of the city threatened an even greater drain on the various budgets.

Pepys may have been overstating the position with his calculation of loss but he, like everyone else, soon became aware that any extensive redesigning and rebuilding of the city was, for the moment, out of the question. The immediate problem became what to do and how to do it?

Parliament dithered and debated, unable to make a decision. Then, in October, the King set up a committee – a commission as it was known – which would debate the situation, survey the burned-out buildings and the streets, then report and make suggestions every week to the King. They were particularly concerned with progress or lack of it. Made up of six individuals, three appointed by the Corporation, three by the King, the commission included men like Sir Christopher Wren and John Hooke.

Using the King's proclamation of 13 September as their baseline, the commission agreed that in any rebuilding or re-designing, narrow streets were to be prohibited, and the quay along the river was to be devoid of any housing. Trades which continually threw out smoke and stinking fumes were also outlawed from the riverside. The commissioners added to these regulations, insisting that the 'new city' should have high streets of 70 feet in width and lesser roads varying between 30 and 40 feet.[4]

The commission debated, Parliament dithered and the King worried. In the meantime, winter inched closer and very little had been done to alleviate the situation for the burned-out residents of London.

* * *

As autumn turned to winter and homeless people in the fields around the city died from disease and exposure, it was apparent that decisions about housing and rebuilding would soon have to be made. For several months debate and discussion had been followed, believe it or not, by even more debate and discussion. Decisions were constantly shelved or delayed and nobody seemed willing to abandon their preconceived ideas.

A bleak Christmas beckoned. It was almost the end of the year and still no progress had been made, many suggestions and proposals foundering on the issue of who would pay to repair or rebuild the housing stock. Would it be landlords or their tenants? Most tenancy agreements contained a clause stating that tenants were responsible for repairing and maintaining the buildings. But burned-out houses and property pulled down to create fire breaks? Where did they fit into the programme? Who would pay to replace them?

Above everything there was always the hovering, unanswered question – rebuild or create brand new? Debate continued, thousands continued to sleep out of doors and London's trade rapidly declined. Finally, pragmatism won out.

In early February 1667 a Rebuilding Act was passed by Parliament, ensuring that the city would be rebuilt, not redesigned. There would be some redesigning of houses, churches and the like, but the protection of traditional roadways, notable buildings and old historic sites was assured. They would survive but the total redesign of the city in order to create a brand new complex was out of the question.

All rebuilding would adhere to the old city street plans, albeit accepting and conforming, where possible, to recommendations from the commissioners. Inevitably, there were changes from the original medieval layout but these were relatively minor when compared to the proposed new cities of Wren, Evelyn and the others.

The rebuilt city would have no long and arrow-straight thoroughfares, no rotundas and no grid pattern of criss-crossing streets. The original city layout was to be followed and preserved so that at least a vestige of the old entity should survive. Survive, yes, but it would become a modernised version of London town without the squalor of the slums that had grown in size and number over the years.

The 'new' city would follow the same routes, holding to the same streets and names as its predecessor. It was the cheapest of all options, and the easiest to implement. It was hardly original but, as might be expected, there were to be some alterations or some modernisation of the original medieval layout.

The rebuilt city was to be practical, unlike the jerry-built structures that had been there before. New developments would make the new city a seventeenth-century design rather than the ramshackle conglomeration of buildings that had sprung up over the years. What had made old London an eyesore would become a thing of beauty.

A building programme was set, keeping costs to a minimum and working to a rebuilding period of three years. Due partly to internal emigration, there was a chronic shortage of labourers to carry out the rebuilding but, even so, most of the work on private properties was underway by 1671.

As well as the thousands of houses lost to the flames, many of London's great buildings had also been devastated by the fire. They also needed to be rebuilt. The first 'public' buildings to be rebuilt were the company halls, like Bricklayers' Hall, the Carpenters' Hall and several more. Less than a dozen such buildings had escaped the fire.

The most important new developments were improvements in the fields of hygiene and fire safety. The commissioners' recommendations about the width of streets were implemented. That meant that the warren of alleyways which had previously been such a foul eyesore was wiped away.

Aimed at alleviating both problems, the extra space created by the widened roads reduced the risk of passing on infections and, at the same time, allowed fire engines reasonable access should the need arise.

Under the terms of the Act, wood was not to be used on the exterior of buildings, except for doors and window frames. All new properties were to be made of brick or stone, consigning to history the days of thatched roofs and wattle and daub walls. Overhanging jetties were ruled out and, where possible, all of the houses in a street should be made to actually look the same.

Uniformity in style and design made construction far easier for the limited work force. Houses in the city were designed to be of a standard or regular size, ranging from two, three and four-storey buildings to grand mansions.

When completed, the standard size and style of housing gave the city an attractive and distinctive style that had been sadly lacking in the pre-fire days.

The theory behind uniformity was correct but even so progress was slow. Disputes between tenants and landlords over who was going to pay for the rebuilding were still regular occurrences, with the result that eventually a Fire Court was established to arbitrate and make judgements over disputes and arguments.

From the beginning, judges in the Fire Court took the view that it was the leaseholder's responsibility to pay for restoring burned property. However, they also decided that in the case of the Great Fire of 1666, leaseholders could not be held responsible as the destruction had been caused by an enemy agent. The ghost of Robert Hubert had been conveniently resurrected.

The Fire Court began its work in February 1667, being abolished in December the following year. It was resurrected in 1670, running for a further year, after which time its usefulness was considered to have expired.

By 1671 the rebuilding programme was well in hand although the number of houses, and therefore residents, was well below the figure from pre-fire days. It took many years and a great deal of development for the population of London to recover.

As the Rebuilding Act was passing through the various stages required to make it law, an announcement was made that Christopher Wren had been appointed to the post of Principal Architect and Surveyor General of the rebuilding project for the city.

It was a post that Wren held for thirty years, rebuilding the destroyed churches of the city becoming something of an obsession for him. Using the previous materials, the use of Portland stone for the main walls of the buildings made Wren's churches spectacular.

Wren went on to design and create the new St Paul's Cathedral, something that was not completed until 1710. Wren was then seventy-eight years old but had lost none of his energy. In total he designed and built fifty-seven churches across London. And, of course, he was knighted for his efforts.

* * *

One revolutionary development to emerge with some degree of credit from the debacle of the fire was house insurance, if people could afford it, against fire and other disastrous events. Previously, there had been no mechanism to allow such a scheme and, anyway, the general consensus seemed to be that there was little or no point to insuring yourself against something that might never happen. It would be like hurling gold coins into the Thames.

The Great Fire of London proved that particular theory to be totally wrong. It took time but in 1680, some fourteen years after the fire was extinguished, once people had been able to assess the damage, a London businessman by the name of Nicholas Barbon, along with eleven other associates, founded the world's first fire insurance company.

As far as the Great Fire of London was concerned It was, perhaps, a little like locking the barn door after the horse had bolted but it was a start. For the first time people saw the sense of such a scheme.

Barbon was a property developer and a proponent of the free market economy. He was unscrupulous and motivated by anything that would guarantee him a quick profit. To do that, he was not afraid of going up against the powers of authority, head-to-head encounters which usually left him the winner.

His development of Red Lion Square in Holborn is a classic example of this type of conflict. Barbon did not have permission to redevelop and build housing in the area but he went ahead regardless of what the Corporation might say or do.

It was inevitable that London Corporation would react, firstly by giving their labour force free reign to challenge the interlopers. Barbon's own workers happily took up the challenge. Fist fights broke out across Holborn and, eventually, the Corporation referred the matter to court. Barbon ignored the threat, treated the matter with contempt and was allowed to continue.

Barbon's career, amongst many other projects, saw him found the National Land Bank. It went bust, showing that even Nicholas Barbon was not immune to the vagaries of the economic markets. However, the creation of the house insurance scheme was the one that secured Barbon a place in history. As if that wasn't enough, he was also the man who physically joined the city of London to the seat of government at Westminster. He did this by building houses on the stretch of open ground that separated the two elements of London.

Nicholas Barbon was a profiteer and a man who had what can be called a quick eye for a good deal, someone who would ride roughshod over people he considered to be weaker than him.

At the time of his death Barbon had financed, established and run developments to the tune of £200,000, a sum that equates to over £35,000,000 in today's money. He was one of many entrepreneurs and men of business who made Stuart London such a dynamic, if not always strictly legal, environment.[5]

Chapter 12

There's a Ghost in the House

Even now, London is, like most long established and ancient cities, a community rife with ghost stories, lurid tales of horror and haunting. Even an event like the Great Fire had its spectral moments, spawning images that still linger and hover on the edge of truth.

However, as far as the Great Fire is concerned there are no terrifying tales of ghostly figures walking in the moonlight or mystical sightings in dark and echoing alleyways. The Tower of London has enough of those to entertain any of the legion of ghost hunters and keep them happy for years. The Tower's ghostly appearances range from the two Princes in the Tower to Anne Boleyn and Sir Walter Raleigh. But instead of such appearances, what the fire provides is a deep-set feeling of unease and horror, something that is often far more terrifying than the traditional ghost sightings and stories.

It begins, naturally enough, with the year of the fire, 1666. According to the Book of Revelations the Number of the Beast, Satan if you prefer, is 666. Religious zealots like the Fifth Monarchists and the Anabaptists seized on the last three digits as a sign or symbol of God's intention of dealing with the unholy city of London.

Humphrey Smith and several others had predicted a dramatic ending for London, making sure that the year 1666 was stressed. It was to be a fiery end, Smith proclaimed, a retribution for decades of debauchery and self-indulgence by the city's inhabitants and an inability by the authorities to control the people they were supposed to govern.

Smith was a Quaker seer who, after his conversion in 1654, abandoned his profession as a well-off farmer and spent much of his later life preaching in a wide variety of locations across England. It was a time of religious intolerance and the Quakers, like the Catholics, were strictly controlled and often punished for their activities and beliefs.

In 1658 Smith was charged with misdemeanour for preaching at a Quaker meeting in Andover. He was sentenced to be held in prison until he gave his word that he would abandon his preaching and adhere to good behaviour. That was not forthcoming and for some time Humphrey Smith stood on his dignity. He lingered long in Winchester prison.

It was a harsh punishment, Smith being detained in a dark and unlighted cell with little or no contact with the outside world. He was not idle in his captivity, however. He wrote several pamphlets and books before he was finally released in 1660.

On his release Humphrey Smith produced his most famous work, a booklet entitled *A Vision Concerning London*. This was published in 1666, a few months before the fire, the most renowned part of the book being his prediction of disaster 'for the city herself and all her suburbs.'[1]

Many religious groups took Smith's words as gospel truth. The Fifth Monarchists in particular saw the raging fire that Smith prophesised as a justifiable end for a sad, sick community.

The Fifth Monarchists were a radical religious group, active during the Commonwealth but virtually dead in the water by 1660. However, there were small groups of adherents still active in England and Wales. These remaining Fifth Monarchists saw the Restoration of the Stuart Monarchy as something that was preventing one of their chief goals, the establishment of the Kingdom of God on Earth.

Renowned figures like Praise God Barebone, Major Thomas Harrison and the Welsh preachers Morgan Llwyd and Vavasor Powell were all either members of the Fifth Monarchy sect or great supporters. Either way, they read and approved Humphrey Smith's work as a revolutionary and totally accurate prophesy.

Smith did not give up preaching, continuing to roam and speak wherever he could. He was eventually arrested once more, after a meeting in Hampshire, and died from gaol fever in Winchester prison in the spring of 1663. That was three years before his predicted disaster but his book and his prophesy lived on after him.

* * *

The other hugely significant prophet of doom and disaster for London was William Lilly, a renowned astrologer. The subject of astrology was then regarded as a science and Lilly was one of its most profound exponents.

In 1651 he had published a book of astrological hieroglyphs, a volume that many claimed to predict the fire. Lilly was reluctant to openly acknowledge this but the book, *Monarchy or No Monarchy in England*, was acclaimed by all sections of society. And popular opinion and acceptance of the contents went far beyond the book's title.

Lilly was believed by many to be a silent member of Colonel John Rathbone's attempt to dethrone the King in April 1666. He had always been a Republican but since the Restoration of the Stuart monarchy in 1660 he was something of a sleeping one.

He joined the plot, many of Lilly's followers believed, with the intention of helping Rathbone by setting fire to the city. And his reason? In order to confirm his reputation as one of the country's leading astrologers. As Lilly already held that position it is difficult to see what he was supposed to achieve by joining Rathbone in his uprising – which was, in any case, doomed before it even began.

Born in 1602, son of a well-off farmer, William Lilly was educated at John Brinsley's renowned grammar school in Ashby de la Zouch. There he learned to read and write in Latin, essential skills for anyone interested in astrology or any of the sciences.

After finishing his schooling, Lilly moved to London where, after a period as servant and secretary to Gilbert White, he moved up in the world. On his employer's death he inherited both the house and White's wife and in 1644 published his first book of astrological prophesy.

His most important work, *Monarchy or No Monarchy in England*, was a book of astrological codes, effectively a collection of horoscopes relating to life in England. There was, of course, a reference – albeit coded – to the Great Fire of London which, it was prophesised, would come in 1666.

Lilly's book was hugely successful, albeit appealing to an audience that was already 'converted.' But nothing was done, the fire destroyed most of the city and astrologers like Lilly were left shaking their heads. When the committee to investigate the fire was set up in the autumn of 1666, Lilly found himself summoned for questioning and interrogation.

He denied making prophesies about the exact date of the destruction which was to come, claiming that his forecasts were not precise and most certainly did not highlight the exact year of the disaster: 'Having found, Sir, that the City of London should be sadly afflicted with as great plague and not long after with an exorbitant fire, I framed these two hieroglyphics as represented in the book, which in effect proved very true.'[2]

He was lying, protecting himself and his reputation. Later examination of the particular drawing related to the fire showed that Lilly had included two children, representing Gemini, the traditional ruler of London. At their feet, other depictions showed scenes of burning buildings. When the page was turned on its side the Roman numerals IXV appeared – IX representing the 9th month, V the 5th and last day of the fire.

The committee accepted Lilly's explanations and a highly relieved William Lilly was thanked for his evidence and dismissed.

* * *

Smith and Lilly were not the only prophets of doom to forecast the destruction of London. There were more, some famous, others of little reputation.

Nostradamus, perhaps the most famous of all forecasters, predicted that, to use his words 'the blood of the just would be demanded.' A French seer and astrologer, Nostradamus had drifted away from standard religion towards the occult after spending a period in Italy.

In 1555 he made nearly one thousand prophesies about the future, amongst other things seeming to predicting the rise of Adolf Hitler and the Nazi Party, the explosion of the French Revolution and the Great Fire of London. The city would be destroyed by fire, he wrote, the disaster occurring in the year 1666. By then, of course, Nostradamus was long dead but his beliefs and his predictions were believed by many.

Even Mother Shipton, the Yorkshire seer, witch or wise woman and prophet, had predicted that disaster would overcome the city. She also claimed it would occur in 1666. When the fire broke out in September 1666 many of London's residents refused to help put out the fire because of her words and simply got out of London while they still could. Claiming that the city would be reduced to ashes, Mother Shipton declared that: 'It was written in the great book of fate that London was to be destroyed.'[3]

Once they had time to think, ordinary citizens found ways of explaining away the fire. Many of their ideas and notions had decidedly satanic overtones.

At the same time as Frenchman Robert Hubert was hanged for his supposed arson attack, in one area of London an effigy of the Pope was burned at the stake. Fair enough. But the head of the effigy was stuffed full of cats. As the flames grew fiercer, the screams from the unfortunate, doomed animals could be heard for miles around. The crowd roared its support; if they couldn't find foreigners to persecute then members of the feline world would have to do.

Hatred of the Dutch, the French and Catholics continued unabated for several years. An anonymous pamphlet published on 5th November 1666 – think about it; the date is significant – claimed that the written material in the pamphlet was the confession of a turncoat Papist who had relented and admitted his guilt. He, the pamphlet declared, had set fire to the city. Nobody could identify the renegade but many believed implicitly in the pamphlet's words.

Stories of strange events and happenings continued to be circulated. One man, John Allin, wrote to a friend stating that the cistern water of Secretary Frith had turned to blood overnight. Water discoloured by debris and broken pipes is easy enough to understand but Allin's next comment, that in Kent it had rained fishes and people had seen hailstones as big as turkey eggs, can only have been the product of imagination run wild.

Even the Spanish Ambassador got in on the act. He reported that a woman in the city had given birth to a deformed monster, part child, part demon, while the fire raged. Groans and screams were apparently heard in London graveyards. Several people reported that, a month or two before the fire, they had seen a pyramid of flame and fire over the sea.

In his diary, Samuel Pepys had already written about the death of London pigeons. Schoolboy William Taswell also put pen to paper to record the melting of lead and copper from the bells and roof of St Paul's Cathedral.

This melting of metal resulted in a cascade of molten lead, copper and brass pouring onto the streets below. The waterfall of metal killed many more birds, coating them in red-hot streams of lead, brass and other materials. The corpses of brass-coated birds were found on Ludgate Hill for many weeks after the event, causing shudders of fear, even terror, to rise up in the hearts of those Londoners who saw them.

Fire in the area around the Tower of London created a vortex that sucked in dung, straw, rags and burned birds. For the citizens of London this was not merely a physical phenomenon, it was also the manifestation of God's unhappiness. It became a story that was used to terrify children for years to come.

Later, towards the end of the nineteenth century, the site of Liverpool Street Station was the centre of ghostly happenings. The station had been built on land that contained mass graves, many of them victims of the plague and some who had died in the aftermath of the Great Fire. Unexplained and sinister noises, shrieks and scratchings were heard at night and a strange feeling of fear descended on the station. Nobody thought that the noises might have come from the new-fangled trains, much easier to blame events of the past.

* * *

As the years progressed and those individuals who had experienced the terrors of the fire inevitably passed away, the roaring flames of those five days in September 1666 stood tall in the imagination of many who came later and had no direct relationship with the event itself. Above everything else, it was fireside stories and tales of the Great Fire that kept the event alive.

As far as society was concerned, lessons were learned, albeit slowly. But the further away the event actually grew, alongside those lessons came the myths that tended to linger far longer than the truth.

Perhaps the greatest falsehood, one that is still remembered and sometimes still taught in schools, is the belief that the Great Fire of London ended the appearance of the bubonic plague in the city and in other parts of the country.

The Black Death had descended on London the year before the Great Fire. It was the last time the plague hit Britain although it continues to attack distant and relatively undeveloped Third World nations across the globe.

It has been reported that some 56,558 citizens of London died during the epidemic, which lasted for eighteen months. In a regular and seemingly unstoppable march of horror, the Black Death swept across the city. Nobody was safe, nobody immune to its tentacles. The King and his Court left London, Parliament closed, trade stuttered to a standstill.

Samuel Pepys and John Evelyn both sent their families away to the country for safety even though the death toll in the provinces was actually higher than that of London. Despite that little-known fact, by the time the epidemic finally died away, it had taken with it approximately half of London's population.

The last few plague deaths occurred in the middle of 1666, just weeks before the fire engulfed the areas where the pandemic had been at its height. Thomas Vincent described the regularity and the terrifying insistence of the Black Death: 'In July [1665] the Plague increaseth, and prevaileth exceedingly, the number of 470, which died in one week by the disease, ariseth to 472 the next week, to 10089 the next, to 1843 the next, to 2010 the next. Now the plague compasseth the walls of the city like a flood.'[4]

Plague, or the Black Death as it was known, had been a regular visitor to British shores since 1348, killing thousands every time it made a visitation. In total it is estimated that bubonic plague, along with its companion pneumonic plague, killed off half of Europe's population in its various visits. Slowly, gradually, however, the visitations of the Black Death were reduced, the disease appearing, firstly, every two or three years and then, by 1666, approximately once in every decade.

Nobody knew its exact cause, everything from divine intervention to infection of the earth being suggested. At the time nobody realised that the disease was passed on to humans by the bite of a flea or louse which had lost its preferred carrier, creatures such as rats.

The myth begins accurately enough, declaring that the fire killed off the rats on which the fleas lived. That is fair enough but then the fantasy begins. There was, the myth declares, no home for rats and fleas in a newly cleansed city, hence the disappearance of the Black Death. Nothing could be further from the truth.

The filthy conditions of virtually all the city streets of Europe were at the heart of the problem. The mounds of human and animal excrement that, before and after the fire, littered the roadways and pavements like mini mountains was what had caused much of the problem. Animals wandered up and down the walkways, defecating where they wished. Householders dumped their refuse and waste when and where they liked. The stench was awful and, more significantly, provided a ready home for disease.

Large cities like London and Paris were ideal targets for the variety of deadly diseases that afflicted communities in the Middle Ages. Streets in the French capital were even being named after human waste. Rue de Merde – *merde* being the French for shit – was a classic example.

The Great Fire of London did not stop the problem of dumping waste in the streets; as Alexander Pope described in his poem *The Alley*, it simply made it worse. For a long while, until the redevelopment of the city began to take effect, it seemed as if nothing had changed.

The fire had, of course, killed off many of the city's rats. However, post-fire, semi-derelict London continued to be an ideal breeding ground for rodents, lice and fleas. They returned in even greater numbers once the flames had finished their work. There is simply no truth in the belief that the fire killed off all the city's rats and fleas.

Only improved hygiene could help in ending the almost annual visitation of the *Yersinia pestis* bacterium, to give the Black Death its correct name. And improved hygiene, without the authorities knowing it, was one of the real reasons for the decline in diseases like the Black Death.

Despite the privations of the coming Jacobite era – and there were to be plenty of those – better personal hygiene, better housing and better sanitation were all brought into Europe's cities, London included.

To begin with, the mounds of waste were still there and would remain in place for some time. But gradually the dumps and the practices that had created them in the first place were removed. Pigs, cattle, ducks and other fowl were also taken out of the picture and stopped from wandering the city streets. Bathing and personal cleanliness, for years decried by the Church and by the civic authorities, slowly became accepted practice.

On a more immediate level, one of the little-known but most effective methods for dealing with infectious diseases were establishments known as pest houses.

Effectively isolation hospitals, these houses were used for keeping plague victims apart from the rest of society. Some of the most effective houses had medical practitioners attached to them while others relied on family and friends to provide care. Soon every city and community of note in England, Scotland and Wales had at least one such establishment.

Quarantine, improved medical services and what can be best termed 'modernisation' played an important part, an essential part, in defeating the plague. It was a gradual process, one not guaranteed success. The fact that the Black Death did not return to London and that the city therefore still stands is proof that the measures taken by the authorities were totally successful.

Ghosts and visitations were left to the imagination and to the fertile brains of writers like John Dryden, who wrote that the traitors to the Crown, men beheaded, their skulls impaled upon London Bridge, were the only ones to rejoice at the fire and its effects:

> The ghost of traitors from the bridge descend,
> With bold, fanatic spectres to rejoyce.
> About the fire into a dance they bend.[5]

There were several other reasons for the last appearance of the Black Death in Britain but they certainly did not include the Great Fire of London. The myth, however, remains.

Epitaph

The Great Fire of London was one of the most dangerous problems or disasters ever to hit England's capital city. It was a disaster of such magnitude that it has, in all probability, been matched only by the Nazi bombing campaign of the Second World War.

The Great Fire destroyed houses and churches. It killed people, probably more than we will ever know if we take into account the death toll of the homeless in the months after the fire. It was, ultimately, the lynchpin for the beginning of our modern world.

What makes the fire and its consequences so fascinating is not the series of events, before and after the blaze, but the people who fought the flames or fled the city. We know who they are and what they did. They are the central focus of this book and so they should be. I make no apologies for that. People and community: they are what all good stories should be about.

Think about the plethora of crime or detective stories to be found on our television screens. Or maybe the soap operas that rival them for popularity. It does not matter where they are set – in the Caribbean or on a railway train from Istanbul, in an isolated rural village or on an island miles from civilisation – in order to make their mark they all depend on people and a sense of community.

These twin factors are always needed to achieve literary success. How the characters deal with the problems they are set, how they use their personalities and the other members of their community to succeed or fail, that is what makes the story successful. It doesn't matter where or how permanent the community might be, as long as it is there to help or hinder. And it is the same with factual tales.

The historical stories that we remember best are not about events but the people they describe and how they deal with the problems – place, people, problem, all drawn and set in a community, that is what makes the topic appealing and interesting.

Those factors are exactly what the Great Fire of London presents to us. Everything else – the progress of the fire, the effects and its consequences – are secondary to the people who had to deal with them. They are what make the history of the Great Fire of London so fascinating.

Notes

Chapter 1. Before the Blaze

1. Adrian Tinniswood, *The Great Fire of London* (2016), pp. 14–15.
2. Stephen Porter, *The Great Fire of London* (1996), p. 11.
3. Ian Mortimer, 'Charles II's revolution,' in *BBC History Magazine*, April 2017, p. 38.
4. Thomas Vincent, *God's Terrible Voice in the City* (1811), p. 40.
5. Ibid., p. 39.
6. Samuel Pepys, *The Diary of Samuel Pepys* Vol. VII (1972), p. 271.
7. John Evelyn, *Diary and Correspondence* Vol. 2 (2006), p. 71.
8. *The London Gazette*, 8 September 1666, p. 1.
9. Ibid.
10. Ibid.

Chapter 2. A Woman Could Piss it Out

1. Samuel Wiseman, *A Short and Serious Narrative on the Burning of London* (1667).
2. Tinniswood, *The Great Fire of London*, p. 7.
3. Evelyn, *Diary and Correspondence*, p. 21.
4. John Evelyn, quoted in Tinniswood, *The Great Fire of London*, p. 74.
5. William Taswell, *Autobiography and Anecdotes*, quoted in Peter Berresford Ellis, *The Great Fire of London* (1976), p. 26.
6. Evelyn, *Diary and Correspondence*, pp. 70–71.

Chapter 3. A View From the Window

1. Pepys, *The Diary of Samuel Pepys*, p. 84.
2. Ibid., p. 85.
3. Vincent, *God's Terrible Voice in the City*, p. 46.
4. https://en.wikipedia.org/wiki/Great_Fire_of_London
5. Vincent, *God's Terrible Voice in the City*, p. 81.
6. https://wikipedia.org/wiki/Flashover
7. Pepys, *The Diary of Samuel Pepys*, p. 86.
8. Ibid.
9. Ibid., p. 89.

10. Ibid., p. 90.
11. Vincent, *God's Terrible Voice in the City*, p. 42.
12. Evelyn, *Diary and Correspondence*, p. 76.
13. Pepys, *The Diary of Samuel Pepys*, p. 93.
14. John Dryden, *Annus Mirabilis* (2016).

Chapter 4. Day Two, the King, the Duke and Samuel Pepys

1. Pepys, *The Diary of Samuel Pepys*, p. 91.
2. Evelyn, *Diary and Correspondence*, p. 71.
3. Quoted in Porter, *The Great Fire of London*, p. 71.
4. Vincent, *God's Terrible Voice in the City*, pp. 75–6.
5. *The London Gazette*, 8 September 1666.
6. Vincent, *God's Terrible Voice in the City*, p. 76.
7. Pepys, *The Diary of Samuel Pepys*, pp. 97–8.
8. Tinniswood. *The Great Fire of London*, p. 57.
9. Vincent, *God's Terrible Voice in the City*, pp. 46–7.

Chapter 5. The Fire Leaps Forward

1. Evelyn, *Diary and Correspondence*, pp. 72–3.
2. https://www.historyhit.com/facts-about-the-great-fire-of-London
3. Pepys, *The Diary of Samuel Pepys*, p. 90.
4. Ellis, *The Great Fire of London*, p. 60.
5. Evelyn, *Diary and Correspondence*, pp. 69–70.
6. Tinniswood, *The Great Fire of London*, pp. 31–2.
7. Vincent, *God's Terrible Voice in the City*, p. 49.
8. https://www.oxbowbooks.com/Blog/2011/02/08
9. Pepys, *The Diary of Samuel Pepys*, p. 90.
10. *The London Gazette*, 8 September 1666.

Chapter 6. Wednesday, Thursday, Good and Bad

1. https://en.wikipedia.org/wiki/Thomas-Bloodworth
2. Taswell, *Autobiography and Anecdotes*, p. 52.
3. Evelyn, *Diary and Correspondence*, p. 58.
4. Vincent, *God's Terrible Voice in the City*, p. 59.
5. Ibid., p. 51.
6. William Taswell, quoted in www://en.wikipedia.org/wiki/William-Taswell.
7. https://Rolls-of-Mortality
8. https://history-in-numbers
9. Pepys, *The Diary of Samuel Pepys*, p. 98.
10. Vincent, *God's Terrible Voice in the City*, p. 53.
11. Ibid., p. 53.
12. https://Rolls-of-Mortality

13. Pepys, *The Diary of Samuel Pepys*, p. 283.
14. Ibid., p. 288.

Chapter 7. Victims, Villains and Heroes

1. Pepys, *The Diary of Samuel Pepys*, p. 98.
2. Vincent, *God's Terrible Voice in the City*, p. 37.
3. Pepys, *The Diary of Samuel Pepys*, p. 97.
4. https://17thcenturyfmp.my blog.arts.ac.uk
5. Wiseman, *A Short and Serious Narrative on the Burning of London.*
6. Pepys, *The Diary of Samuel Pepys*, p. 87.
7. Ibid., pp. 102–3.
8. Evelyn, *Diary and Correspondence*, pp. 75–6.
9. Pepys, *The Diary of Samuel Pepys*, p. 94.
10. Ibid., pp. 96–7.
11. https://www.poetryexplorer.net/poem.php?id=10052112
12. Ibid.

Chapter 8. Surveying the Damage

1. Quoted in Ellis, *The Great Fire of London*, p. 100.
2. Ellis, *The Great Fire of London*, p. 78.
3. Poem by John Crouch, quoted in Ellis, *The Great Fire of London*, p. 64.
4. Evelyn, *Diary and Correspondence*, p. 90.
5. Ibid., p. 76.
6. Vincent, *God's Terrible Voice in the City*, pp. 92–3.
7. Ellis, *The Great Fire of London*, p. 104.
8. https://www.bing.com/search?q=James+hickes
9. *The London Gazette*, 10 September 1666.
10. https://www.bing.com/search?q=James+hickes

Chapter 9. Post Debacle Efforts – Remembering the Fire

1. https://encylopaedia.org/wiki/Vauxhall-Gardens
2. James Boswell, *The Life of Samuel Johnson* (1993), p. 599.
3. Letter from Henry Griffith to his cousin, quoted in Ellis, *The Great Fire of London*, p. 6.
4. Jo Morgan, quoted in *BBC History Magazine.*
5. https://en.wikipedia.org/wiki/Great-Fire-of -London
6. Pepys, *The Diary of Samuel Pepys*, p. 98.
7. Children's Poem – Public Domain.
8. Ellis, *The Great Fire of London*, p. 76.
9. Ellis, *The Great Fire of London*, p. 100.
10. Dryden, *Annus Mirabilis.*
11. Wiseman, *A Short and Serious Narrative on the Burning of London.*

12. Dryden, *Annus Mirabilis.*
13. https://en.wikipedia.org/wiki/Great-Fire-of-London

Chapter 10. Remember, Rember the Second of September

1. 'An Humble Remonstrance to the King and Parliament,' quoted in Ellis, *The Great Fire of London*, p. 112.
2. Ellis, *The Great Fire of London*, p. 92.
3. Message on commemorative plaque now held in the Guildhall Museum.
4. https://enwikipedia/wiki/ the Great Fire
5. Vincent, *God's Terrible Voice in the City*, p. 53.
6. Porter, *The Great Fire of London*, p. 78.
7. Alexander Pope, 'The Alley,' in *Collected Poems* (1983), p. 3.

Chapter 11. A New City, A new Concept

1. Letter, John Evelyn to Sir Samuel Tuke, included in Evelyn, *Diary and Correspondence.*
2. Porter, *The Great Fire of London*, p. 102.
3. Pepys, *The Diary of Samuel Pepys*, pp. 108–9.
4. Porter, *The Great Fire of London*, p. 108.
5. Ellis, *The Great Fire of London*, p. 90.

Chapter 12. There's a Ghost in the House

1. Humphrey Smith, *A Vision Concerning London* (1660).
2. https://en.wikipedia.org/wiki/Great-Fire-of-London
3. https://archive.org/details/bim-early-english-works
4. Thomas Vincent, *God's Terrible Voice in the City*, p. 13.
5. Dryden, *Annus Mirabilis.*

Bibliography

Primary Sources

Dryden, John, *Annus Mirabilis*, London 1667, reprinted 2016, Portable Poetry, London

Evelyn, John, *Diary and Correspondence*, Vol. 2, re-published by Project Gutenberg, November 2006

Pepys, Samuel, *Diary*, Vol. VII, published by G. Bell & Sons, London, 1972

Smith, Humphrey, *A Vision Concerning London*, privately printed and published 1660, London

Taswell, William, *Autobiography and Anecdotes*, edited by Elliot, published 1853

Vincent, Thomas, *God's Terrible Voice in the City*, published by Jackson, 1668, re-published by Lockwood, London, 1811

Wiseman, Samuel, *A Short and Serious Narrative on the Burning of London*, poem, published 1667, London

Secondary Sources – Books

Boswell, James, *The Life of Samuel Johnson*, London, 1790. Republished by Barnes & Noble and in Everyman's Editions, January 1993

Careba, Erica, *The Commendable Life and Noble Death of Humphrey Smith*, Unpublished PhD Thesis, University of Birmingham, undated

Carey, John (ed.), *The Faber Book of Reportage*, Faber, London, 1987

Ellis, Peter Berresford, *The Great Fire of London*, New English Library, London, 1976

Swift, Jonathan, *Gulliver's Travels*, Collins, London, 2010

Tinniswood, Adrian, *The Great Fire of London*, Vintage Classics, Penguin, London, 2016

Pope, Alexander, *Collected poems*, JM Dent, London, 1983

Porter, Stephen, *The Great Fire of London*, Bramley, Godalming, 1996

Secondary Sources – Newspapers/Magazines

BBC History Magazine, Jan 2017 – August 2024

The London Gazette, 8 September 1666

The London Gazette, 10 September 1666

History Today, various issues

Quaker Studies, Vol. 25, No. 1

Secondary Sources – TV/Films and Videos
The Great Fire of London (Amazon Prime Video).
Great Fire of London: The Untold Story (National Geographic).

Websites
https://en.wikipedia.org/wiki/Great-Fire-of-London
https://www.london-fire.gov.uk/museum/history
https://www.historyhit.com/facts-about-the-great-fire-of-london
https://en.wikipedia.org/wiki/Thomas-Bloodworth
https://wn.wikipedia.org/William-Taswell
https://www.oxbowbooks.com/blog/2017/02/08
https://historyinnumbers/comp/events/fire-of-london
https://billsofmortality.org
https://enencylopaedia.org/wiki/Vauxhall-Gardens
https://www.skyscript.co.uk, fire
https://quakerstudies.open libhums.org/article